THOMISTIC PAPERS
V

THOMISTIC PAPERS
V

Thomas A. Russman, OFM Cap
Editor

CENTER FOR THOMISTIC STUDIES
University of St. Thomas
3812 Montrose Boulevard
Houston, Texas 77006

NIHIL OBSTAT:
Reverend Terence P. Brinkman, S.T.D.
Censor Deputatus

IMPRIMATUR:
Most Reverend Joseph A. Fiorenza
Bishop of Galveston-Houston
April 6, 1990

LC 83-73623
ISBN 0-268-01875-8 (cloth)
ISBN 0-268-01876-6 (paper)

Manufactured in the United States of America

CONTENTS

INTRODUCTION

This issue of *Thomistic Papers* can be divided into two parts. The first is made up of pieces which connect more or less directly with the philosophical work of Etienne Gilson. In the first of these pieces John Knasas rejects the widely held view that Gilson theologized metaphysics. Any religious believer who does philosophy in a wholehearted way will surely find that his religious convictions influence his philosophical choices and directions at key points. But when does this influence transform what he or she is doing from metaphysics into theology? Knasas does not shrink from the subtlety required to answer this question; he insists that in the end both Gilson and Thomas argue metaphysics philosophically rather than theologically, although they gratefully accept hints from revelation as to where these arguments might be found and where they might lead. The hints may be theological, but the foundation and execution of argument are philosophical.

In the second Gilson article, Armand Maurer discusses Gilson's view that the history of ideas can be used by the philosopher as a domain for "metaphysical experimentation." One could restate Gilson's point in Popperian terms: Just as scientific experimentation functions as an attempt to falsify a scientific theory by putting it to the test, so the fully worked out consequences by later thinkers of a major philosophical principle can bring to light consequences that count against that principle. Gilson admits that such dialectical procedures cannot in themselves deliver positive truth, but insists they can serve to narrow the field of possibilities for consideration. Gilson goes so far as to claim that, given the nature of the human mind, such historical dialectic is indispensable in pursuing philosophical truth. Intuition, insight, and the arguments based upon them are the route to positive truth; but the vacillating and error-prone human intellect needs to be buttressed all around by dialectic, if it is to find and hold the truth with assurance.

Maurer's article is followed by an Appendix, the first published translation into English of the key article by Gilson concerning the above. Maurer himself did the translation with some help from William Young and Thomas A. Russman.

Leonard Kennedy's article is a fitting third piece for this first part. It explores one particular historical example of a strong interconnection between theology and philosophy, and it uses the method of historical experimentation as a vindication of philosophical and theological truth. In its turn, Kennedy's article can be seen as an experiment on the method of historical experimentation whose principles Gilson and Maurer have placed before us.

The second part of this volume deals with the relationship between philosophy and faith. It is full of dialectical arguments and references to important historical figures; but the series of dialectical experiments takes place in the present, and in the end is left incomplete. The format of the discussion is new to *Thomistic Papers*. Thomas Sullivan begins with a revised version of his 1989 Aquinas Lecture given at the University of St. Thomas. How does the believer arrive at the certainty of faith? How do the intellect and will interact in the process? And where is the sufficiency of the Holy Spirit needed and supplied? Sullivan has a very useful way of presenting these problems as he argues for one line of solution. Russman's reply seems to raise serious concerns about parts of Sullivan's argument and suggests a rather different line for a solution.

By prior agreement, the format called for Sullivan to have the last word, albeit a brief one. Here, however, the earlier vigorous promise of the discussion sputters, with Sullivan claiming that Russman has misunderstood him. One advantage of the format is that the reader is able to decide for himself who has misunderstood whom. And one hopes the reader is left with something more valuable—a well set up invitation to pursue the series of dialectical experiments further. Certainly one hopes that Sullivan and Russman will find opportunities to continue their discussion.

***

Thomistic Papers goes to press on an occasional basis. The Editor welcomes contributions that are appropriate for a series of this title and would be pleased to entertain proposals to edit an entire volume of *Thomistic Papers* around a single topic (as was done in *Thomistic Papers IV*).

The Editor

DOES GILSON THEOLOGIZE THOMISTIC METAPHYSICS?*

John F. X. Knasas

By way of introduction let me define the terms of the question. By "Thomistic metaphysics" I understand the philosophical science whose subject is *ens inquantum ens*, especially as *ens* is understood as *habens esse*—a possessor of the act of existence. By "theologize" I mean the attempt to base one's position on a point logically inaccessible to natural reason but accessible to religious faith. By "natural reason" I intend intellectual capacity as it is common to religious believer and unbeliever. Finally, by "Gilson" I mean both the man and the logic of his ideas. Hence, in sum my question is: "Does either Gilson himself or the logic of his ideas rest the attainment of Aquinas' science of *ens inquantum ens* on a point accessible to religious faith alone?"

Various authors claim that Gilson intends just such a thing. In his *Metaphysics and the Existence of God*, Thomas C. O'Brien argues that Gilson identifies the *de facto* development of Thomistic metaphysics with its doctrinal development.[1] In fact Aquinas came to his existential understanding of being by meditation upon *Ego sum qui sum* of Exodus III, 14. In virtue of two remarks, O'Brien believes that Gilson inflates this historical observation into a doctrinal requirement. First, Gilson insists that the approach to God from creatures is Cartesian.

> Some profess (sic) to reconstruct St. Thomas's teaching in the philosophical order proceeding from things to God rather than in the theological order proceeding from God to things fail to take into consideration the difficulties of such an undertaking... To isolate his philosophy from his theology is to present the philosophical thought of St. Thomas in an arrangement demanded by a philosophy in which everything is "considered by natural reason without the light of faith." (Descartes, *Principes*, Preface, ed. Adam Tannery, IX, 4, 1. 19-20 and 5, 1. 13-18). In brief, it is to present a *philosophia ad mentem sancti Thomae* as though it were a *philosophia ad mentem Cartesii.*[2]

Second, Gilson says that God is the object of metaphysics:

> ...for in raising our thoughts to the consideration of Him Who Is, Christianity revealed to metaphysics the true nature of its proper object. When, with Aristotle, a Christian defines metaphysics as the science of being as being, we may rest assured that he understands it always as the science of Being as Being: *id cujus actus est esse*, that is to say, God.[3]

O'Brien takes the point of these remarks to be that metaphysics must begin with God. Hence, Gilson is theologizing metaphysics.

In his article, "Teaching Metaphysics: The Value of Aquinas for the Seminarian Today," John Wippel draws attention to Gilson's pedagogical insistence that if we are to study Thomistic metaphysics before we are fifty, then we should study Thomistic theology. Gilson remarks:

...if we wish to introduce Christian students
to metaphysics and ethics, to teach them the
relevant parts of his theology will be to provide
them with the best short cut to some understanding
of these disciplines.[4]

Wippel holds that Gilson's procedure contradicts Aquinas' own
metaphysical procedure. Wippel says,

[Aquinas'] metaphysics rather begins with a
metaphysical notion of being as being, which
notion, presumably, is derived from one's
knowledge of concrete sensible entities and
one's application thereto of the twofold type
of judgment we have noted above, a positive
judgment directed towards a thing's *esse*, on
the one hand, required, I would think, even
for one to get to a primitive and non-metaphysical
notion of being, and a negative judgment
or *separatio*, on the other, required to free
one's original notion of being from restriction
to the material and changing. One may debate
Thomas's view as to the presuppositions for
this discovery of being as being and for the
negative judgment or *separatio*. But that
is another matter. For the present it is enough
for us to note that there are ample indications
in Thomas's writings as to his views with
respect to the nature, the subject-matter, and
the method of procedure appropriate to
metaphysics. It would seem, therefore, that
if one wishes to recover the elements of
this metaphysics from Thomas's various writings,
one should present those elements according
to the philosophical order outlined by Thomas
himself, not according to Gilson's proposed
theological order.[5]

Finally, John M. Quinn's critique of Gilson's Christian philosophy thesis also drives home the charge that Gilson theologizes Thomistic metaphysics. In sum, since Thomistic metaphysics is part of what Gilson calls Christian philosophy and since Christian philosophy, upon analysis, is really theology, then Thomistic metaphysics is theology. By "Christian philosophy" is meant that portion of revelation accessible to natural reason and explicated by Aquinas in his theology. In his *The Thomism of Etienne Gilson: A Critical Study*, Quinn gives three arguments that Christian philosophy so taken is actually theology. First, philosophy's handling of truths of faith naturally accessible makes it formally identical with theology.[6] In other words, a philosophy whose subject is revealed data must be non-philosophical. In the same vein, Quinn declares, "Even a Thomas Aquinas discoursing in light of theological truths cannot make anything but a per se contribution to theology."

Second, Quinn challenges Gilson's analogical comparison of Christian philosophy to mathematical physics. In reply Quinn again insists, "The wedding of philosophy to theology...does not beget a philosophical theology or a theological philosophy; applied in theology, an ancillary philosophy yields only theology."[7]

Third, Quinn corrects Gilson's reading of *Aeterni patris*.[8] What the encyclical calls Christian philosophy is philosophizing with faith as an extrinsic norm. What Gilson calls Christian philosophy is the method of scholastic philosophy rightly used in expounding revealed truths. The latter is philosophy as an *ancilla* in theology. What Gilson calls Christian philosophy is really theology.

All three of the above thinkers misread Gilson. O'Brien's two reasons for claiming that Gilson makes Aquinas' *de facto* approach to metaphysics from revelation identical with the doctrinal approach fail to stand scrutiny. What does Gilson have in mind when he denigrates the approach to God from creatures as Cartesian? First, in his *The Christian Philosophy of St. Thomas Aquinas*, from which comes Gilson's remark about Cartesianism, Gilson expressly states that metaphysics comes to a knowledge of God starting from sensible things:

> Now God is a purely spiritual substance.
> Our knowledge, on the contrary, is the acquired
> knowledge proper to a being composed of
> soul and body. It necessarily has its origin
> in the senses. Our knowledge of God, therefore,
> begins with such sense data as we can have
> of a purely intelligible being. Thus our
> understanding, using the testimony of the
> senses as its starting point, can infer that
> God exists.[9]

Second, Gilson stresses that Aquinas "found in his theological investigations an incentive to carry metaphysics beyond the point where his predecessors had left it."[10]   Accordingly, the attempt to release Thomistic philosophy from its theological moorings runs the risk of not knowing its origin or its end, of altering its nature, and even of no longer grasping its meaning. The previous two points in tandem indicate to me that the Cartesian approach Gilson criticizes is not simply the approach to God from creatures but the approach to God from creatures that tries to employ in no way whatsoever, even indirectly, any assistance from revelation.

That this is the Cartesianism Gilson castigates is clear from his essay, "What Is Christian Philosophy?". The essay first appeared in Anton Pegis' *A Gilson Reader* (1957) and is at least contemporaneous with Gilson's *Christian Philosophy of Aquinas* (1956).   In the essay Gilson depicts the Cartesian mode of doing philosophy "in the light of natural reason alone" as intending a strict separation from theology. It was "an attempt to return in Christian times to the pre-Christian position of the problem."[11]   In my own words, the Cartesian attitude is the mother-I'd-rather-do-it-myself approach brought into philosophy. No assistance from revelation is sought, no assistance is desired. In the essay Gilson goes on to say that the Cartesian attitude stands in contrast to the notion of Christian philosophy elaborated in *Aeterni patris*. The encyclical recommends the attitude of

those who "to the study of philosophy unite obedience to the
Christian faith."[12] The assistance that the Christian faith affords
philosophy is illustrated by an analogy given in the *Christian
Philosophy of Aquinas.* Gilson says,

> ...[Aquinas] affirms that, by passing along
> the road of revelation, reason sees truths
> which it might otherwise have overlooked.
> The traveller whom a guide has conducted
> to a mountain peak sees no less of the
> view because another has opened it up for
> him. The panorama is no less real because
> the helping hand of another has brought
> him to it.[13]

Perhaps the chief example of what Gilson is thinking about
here is Aquinas' use of the *Ego sum qui sum* revelation of
Exodus III, 14. According to Gilson, Aquinas understood this
revelation to mean that God is pure existence. As such God's
most proper effect in creatures ought to be the existence of
creatures. This reflection is a case of the "helping hand of
revelation." Brought by revelation to understand that the existence
of a being is a special dimension of it, the philosopher goes
on to see this truth for himself. The hint provided by revelation
does not mitigate in the least a *bona fide* philosophical appropriation
of this truth. As will be noted, Aquinas' philosophical appropriation
of the existential dimension of beings consists in his doctrine
of the *secunda operatio intellectus.* Aquinas' Christian philosophy
is, then, no less a philosophy. Gilson goes on to insist:

> What we call Thomistic philosophy is a body
> of rigorously demonstrable truths and is justifiable
> precisely as philosophy by reason alone. When
> we speak of St. Thomas as of a philosopher,
> it is a question only of his demonstrations.
> It is of little importance that his thesis comes
> right where faith would have it. He never
> calls upon faith, nor asks us to call upon

it in those proofs which he regards as rationally demonstrated.[14]

In conclusion, Gilson castigates the Cartesian attitude not for going from creatures to God but for trying to do that with a deaf ear[15] to revelation. Contrariwise, Gilson's insistence that we proceed from God to creatures has more to do with the helpful hints and suggestions offered to philosophy by revelation than with any theologizing of philosophy. Philosophy must proceed to God from creatures. But it can do that either fortified by revelation or isolated from it.

What of O'Brien's second reason for Gilson's identifying the historical with the doctrinal, viz., Gilson makes God the object of metaphysics? Whatever Gilson intends, the full text shows that Gilson is not making metaphysics start from God instead of creatures. A few lines prior to those designating God as the object of metaphysics, Gilson remarks:

> ...we ought to say that Christian philosophy essentially excludes all merely physical proofs of the existence of God, and admits only physico-metaphysical proofs, that is to say proofs suspended from Being as being.[16]

Being as being is the subject of metaphysics from which God, Being as Being, is reached. Gilson's position here accords perfectly with Aquinas' on the relation of God to the subject of metaphysics and the procedure from the latter to the former.[17] Gilson's calling God the object of metaphysics has nothing to do with theologizing metaphysical procedure.

Wippel's contention that Gilson's pedagogical insistence on using theology to teach metaphysics also misreads Gilson. Wippel confuses a pedagogical technique with the content of what is being taught by the technique. Gilson believes that a theological context enlivens material that would otherwise be abstract and remote to students. Gilson says,

> The main reason of Thomas Aquinas against
> an early teaching of metaphysics was the
> exceedingly abstract nature of its object. Religion
> cannot change it, but religion provides an
> exceedingly concrete approach to certain notions
> which the metaphysician considers in an abstract
> way. To take only one example, I do not
> consider it easy to interest a class of undergraduates
> in the metaphysical notion of "pure act";
> but if you can tell them that what you call
> pure act is another name for God, then they
> will realize that you are talking about something
> they already know, and not about a mere
> word.... All the concreteness conferred by
> religion upon the abstract object of metaphysical
> speculation,. . ., can be considered so many
> favorable conditions for the earlier ripening
> of aptness to philosophical speculation.[18]

Nowhere does Gilson suggest that the pedagogical technique
becomes part of the very thing taught. What is taught is
metaphysics as it proceeds from the being of creatures to its
source in *Ipsum esse*. Effectively teaching the science requires
a theological locus, but the science itself, i.e., what is taught,
does not require theology. Gilson would have no substantial
disagreement with Wippel's presentation of the unfolding of
metaphysics itself.[19] Gilson's overriding interest remains how
to make this metaphysical speculation relevant to Christian students.
A correlation with their religious belief is the answer.

In reply to Quinn, Gilson is quite aware that everything
in the *Summa Theologiae*, for example, is theology. After
all, the title means a summary of theology. Gilson does not
need Quinn to point this out. In fact Gilson's acknowledgment
of the theological character of Aquinas' *Summa* is precisely
what leads him to tackle the issue of why a philosopher ought
to read it. Gilson's answer[20] is that though everything in
the *Summa* is theology, not everything in the *Summa* is only
theology. Sufficient for an item to be theological is that

it be included within revelation. Aquinas' notion of the theological encompasses many truths of natural reason, e.g., God's existence, unicity, and spirituality. God placed them in his revelation to us because they are necessary if salvation is to be accomplished in a sure and fitting manner; due to their difficulty, they would otherwise be known only to a few. Explicating this portion of revelation, the theologian cannot help but philosophize. The explication of a philosophical truth is to philosophize. Hence, even though everything in the *Summa* deals with revelation and so is theology, not all this theology is only theology. Some of the theology is also philosophy. All three of Quinn's arguments are oblivious to this crucial insight.[21]

The same basis can be employed to address Quinn's other critical remarks. Quinn is incorrect to characterize what Gilson calls Christian philosophy as an unthomistic *tertium quid* between philosophy itself and theology.[22] In light of the above, Gilson's Christian philosophy is philosophy itself explicated by a Christian theologian. For example, Aquinas obviously considers the *Quinque Viae* to be theology, for he includes them within his *Summa Theologiae*. But nowhere does he insist, as Quinn does *contra* Gilson, that they are *only* theology. In fact in the first book of the *Summa Contra Gentiles*, where Aquinas is speaking as an expositor of the truth of the Catholic faith, he presents (ch. 13) four of the *viae* as arguments of the philosophers Aristotle and Averroes. Plainly Aquinas fails to regard his theological enterprise as making all that is treated only theology.

Finally, Quinn's complaint that Gilson's notion of Christian philosophy is not just a synthesis of philosophy and theology in the order of exercise but a confusion of the two in the line of specification is also off target. Quinn insists that you cannot have a theologian doing philosophy, and you cannot have philosophy in theology.[23] This last remark makes sense if taken to mean that a theologian cannot be doing only philosophy and that only philosophy is in theology. But as I labored to point out, the Thomistic theologian's doing philosophy is also his doing theology, and the philosophy within Thomistic theology is also theology.

None of the above critics succeed in tarring Gilson as
a theologizer. Nevertheless, the criticism is not yet dead.
There remains a genuinely disconcerting text from Gilson's *The
Elements of Christian Philosophy*. After emphasizing that in
Thomism "existence" does not mean a state of the thing but
an interior act of the thing, Gilson asks how Aquinas achieved
the awareness of the very possibility of this notion. He answers
his own question this way:

> To tell the whole truth, even so-called "Thomists"
> have been and still are divided on this point
> [whether to treat the thing's existence as
> the fact of the thing or as an act of the
> thing]. No such disagreement would take
> place if the presence, in things themselves,
> of an act in virtue of which they can be
> called "being" were a conclusion susceptible
> of demonstration.

> This impasse is an invitation to us to give
> up the philosophical way—from creatures to
> God—and try the theological way—from God
> to creatures. Thomas Aquinas may well
> have first conceived the notion of an act
> of being (*esse*) in connection with God and
> then, starting from God, made use of it
> in his analysis of the metaphysical structure
> of composite substances.[24]

To the defender of Gilson's philosophical integrity, such words
prima facie are an indigestible bit of theologizing. Gilson
appears to settle the Thomistic dispute over *esse* in favor of
esse as act by an appeal to theology.

Is the text *bona fide* theologizing? If it is, then it certainly
was not Gilson's last word on the subject. In the sixth edition
of *Le Thomisme* (1972), Gilson repeats his oft mentioned thesis
that knowledge of *esse* is in and through judgment. Gilson
says,

These two distinct operations both see the
real, but they do not penetrate it to the same
depth: intellection attains the essence, which
the definition formulates, judgment attains the
very act of existing [le jugement atteint
l'acte même d'exister].[25]

Judgment is an act of the human intellect, an intellect common
to believer and unbeliever. Furthermore, in *Le Thomisme*, Gilson
squarely rests Aquinas' metaphysics upon the resources of judgment:

A metaphysics of being, insofar as being
consignifies existence, does not signify existence
unless it precisely uses the second operation
of the understanding and employs all the
resources of judgment. The feeling, so just
in itself, that the universal concept of being
is the contrary of an empty notion, finds
justification here. Its richness consists, first,
of all the judgments of existence it virtually
comprises and connotes,...[26]

In this passage, Gilson is clearly not a theologizer of Thomistic
metaphysics. The metaphysical viewpoint is set up thanks
to the judgments that reveal various things in the light of
their *esses*.

But it is unlikely that *Le Thomisme* signals a change of
Gilson's mind from his *Elements of Christian Philosophy*. For
the latter iterates the same doctrine of judgment.

The second operation, which is the composition
or division of concepts—that is, the judgment—
attains the thing in its very act of being....
This conclusion, so firmly asserted by Thomas
Aquinas, has often been overlooked or
intentionally rejected by many among his
successors. And no wonder, since it is

tied up with the Thomistic notion of the
composition of essence and the act of being
in created substances.[27]

Gilson even insists that the judgmental grasp of *esse* is a
"natural" operation of the human intellect.[28] It is very improbable
that our purported theologizing text means to rule out a philosophical
approach to Aquinas' understanding of existence as *actus essendi*.

What, then, does our text mean? I believe Joseph Owens
is right to interpret it as Gilson surmising how revelation led
Aquinas to a conception of existence that Aquinas went on
to elaborate in straight philosophical fashion.

> The tenet that the being of a thing is originally
> grasped through judgment and not through
> conceptualization seems introduced in the
> theological method of St. Thomas as the
> necessary epistemological support for an already
> accepted notion of God. If such be the
> case, it is entirely possible that St. Thomas
> was led to his metaphysical starting point
> by meditating on a scriptural notion of God,
> interpreted against a Neoplatonic background.
> It may be the case, likewise, that to appreciate
> the philosophical force and understand the
> full metaphysical significance of this tenet,
> the easiest way—perhaps, one might insist,
> the psychologically indicated way—is to retrace
> the steps by which it emerged out of its
> original historic setting at a definite epoch
> of Christian theology. It also may be possible
> to take the stand that other thinkers have
> missed this apparently obvious starting point
> because they did not use the theological
> approach. But with all this stated and weighed,
> the simple fact remains that the tenet is
> presented by St. Thomas as something

> immediately observable. Not the slightest
> indication is given that it is meant as a
> conclusion from other premises, or that any
> religious authority is being appealed to for
> its acceptance.[29]

Indeed, Gilson is speaking not of the *only* way to acknowledge *esse*. His professed intent is to explain how Aquinas "first" came by the notion. As he also remarks: "The problem under discussion now is: how did Thomas Aquinas achieve the awareness of the very possibility of this notion."[30] Gilson's suggested answer is, "Through revelation." Accepting the *Ego sum qui sum* revelation of Exodus III, 14, at its face value, Aquinas understood God as pure *esse*. Such an understanding of God produced an understanding of the existence of things as God's proper effect. Gilson explains:

> It is one and the same thing to conceive
> God as pure *Esse* and to conceive things,
> so far as they *are*, as including in their
> metaphysical structure a participated image
> of the pure Act of Being.[31]

None of Gilson's speculation should mar Gilson's opinion that Aquinas proceeds to elaborate judgment as the philosophical confirmation of a truth offered by revelation.

It is no objection to Owens' interpretation to recall Gilson's claim: "No such disagreement would take place if the presence, in things themselves, of an act in virtue of which they can be called 'being' were a conclusion susceptible of demonstration." A reading of the previous pages shows that the open-ended demonstration that Gilson has in mind is the Avicennian argumentation reiterated by Aquinas in his *De Ente et Essentia*.

> Whatever does not belong to the notion of
> an essence or quiddity comes from without
> and enters into composition with the essence,

for no essence is intelligible without its parts.
Now, every essence or quiddity can be understood
without anything being known of its existing.
I can know what a man or a phoenix is
and still be ignorant whether it exists in
reality. From this it is clear that the act
of existing is other than essence or quiddity,
. . .[32]

Gilson's comment on this argument is that it fails to prove
the distinction between essence and existence in concrete substances.
Why?   Gilson explains:

The argument proves only that, in a created
universe, existence must come to essences
from outside and, therefore, be superadded
to them. Any metaphysics or theology that
recognizes the notion of creation necessarily
agrees on this point. All Christian theologies
in particular expressly teach that no finite
being is the cause of its own existence,
but this does not imply that existence is
created in the finite substance as a distinct
"act of being" (*esse*) added by God to its
essence and composing the substance with
it.[33]

In other words, the reasoning is open-ended because the word
"existence" can be taken either in the *fact* sense or the Thomistic
act sense.   Consequently, the conclusion could mean either
that the fact of existing is other than the essence or that
the act of existing is other than the essence. Instead of demonstrating
the Thomistic sense of existence, the reasoning presupposes
it.   Used as an approach to Thomistic *esse*, it understandably
leads to the stalemate that Gilson describes a few pages later
in our purported theologizing text.

In sum, Gilson's insistence that the Thomistic notion of *esse* is not susceptible to demonstration concerns the above Avicennian/Thomistic text. That seems to be all Gilson is talking about. He is not making any absolute claim, viz., *actus essendi* is philosophically unknowable. Rather, Gilson's words leave the way open for the presentation of judgment as the original philosophical apprehension of *esse*.

In conclusion, I think that it is virtually certain that, despite a fairly popular conception to the contrary, Gilson the man never intends to theologize Thomistic metaphysics. Taken in context, his insistence upon the benefits of revelation for reason is not meant to supplant or preclude an authentically philosophical development of the science. The philosophical development begins with the judgmental grasp of the *esses* of sensible things, moves to an apprehension of *ens* in the *habens esse* sense, and completes itself in the demonstration of *Ipsum Esse*. Some might still wish to fault if not Gilson the man, then at least the logic of his ideas. In particular, a shortcoming in Gilson's portrayal of judgment continues to create the suspicion that an appeal to revelation is a necessity for metaphysics. I would like to finish by briefly addressing this shortcoming.

Gilson at least gives the impression of equating the judgment with the proposition. For example, "Existential judgments are meaningless unless they are meant to be true. If the proposition, 'Peter is,' means anything, it means that a certain man, Peter by name, actually is, or exists."[34] Also, "The formula in which this composition is expressed is precisely the proposition or judgment."[35] Such an equation is unfortunate because judgment is supposed to be the intellectual act that *grasps* the *esse rei*, while the proposition at best only *expresses esse*. As Aquinas himself points out, the enunciation, or proposition, signifies the *esse rei* that the *secunda operatio intellectus* grasps (*respicit*).[36] The result of Gilson's equating of the judgment with the proposition is the appearance of an undeveloped notion of the intellectual act of judgment itself that "*respicit esse rei*."

This shortcoming can be handled by two remarks. First, Aquinas generally describes the cognitional act of judgment this way: "Our intellect composes or divides by applying previously abstracted intelligibles to the thing."[37]

This description enables the reader to understand that the intellect's second act of composition and division is what Aquinas elsewhere describes as the intellect's indirect knowledge of singular existents. Such knowledge is attained by a certain reflection, *per quandam reflexionem*, back from the universal to the phantasm from which the universal had been abstracted and in which the individual is represented.[38] Actually Gilson is fully aware of what I am identifying as judgment. In his *Thomist Realism and the Critique of Knowledge*, Gilson says: "Thus, for St. Thomas the problem of the existential judgment is linked to the analogous problem of the apprehension of the singular."[39] Gilson describes Aquinas' position on the intellect's indirect knowledge of the singular.[40] The problem here is to explain how this can happen. Gilson's solution is to distinguish the Thomistic conception of man from the Cartesian. Unlike Descartes for whom man is a mysterious union of the two substances of mind and body, Aquinas conceives man as a single substance that both senses and understands. Thomistic anthropology undergirds a commerce between sense and intellection that permits the intellect's indirect knowledge of the singular existent. But despite the importance of the material for understanding judgment itself, Gilson continues to distinguish it from judgment. As noted, existential judgment is only "linked," not identified, with the intellect's indirect apprehension of singular existents. The reader of Gilson, however, can make this correction. Once made, Gilson's presentation of Aquinas' doctrine of judgment is more full-bodied than suggested by the propositional account.

Second, the task remains of explaining how judgment in the described cognitional operation sense is a *respicit esse rei* rather than simply the recomposition of an intelligible with some designated matter. As far as I know, Gilson nowhere performs this task. The task, however, can be accomplished and the Thomistic texts themselves provide the help. In sum, they describe a consideration of the individual material thing itself as *possibile esse et non esse.*[41] Such a consideration appears to be generated from data comprised of the thing really existing, on the one hand, and the real thing cognitionally existing on the other.[42] The consideration of the individual body as possible permits judgment to recombine the abstracted intelligible with the individual in a fashion that leaves the recomposition of the individual with its *esse* as a further distinct and crowning moment in judgment.

An elaboration of these two remarks, I believe, strengthens the logic of Gilson's position on the philosophical approach to metaphysics. Hence, not only in intention but also in idea, Gilson is no theologizer of Thomistic metaphysics.

*This article is also forthcoming in the *Atti del IX Congresso Tomistico Internazionale* under the auspices of the Roman Pontifical Academy of St. Thomas.

University of St. Thomas
Houston, Texas

NOTES

1. Thomas C. O'Brien, *Metaphysics and the Existence of God* (Washington: The Thomist Press, 1960), 121-2, 187.

2. Etienne Gilson, *The Christian Philosophy of St. Thomas Aquinas* (New York: Random House, 1956), n. 33, 442-3. Apparently Gilson intended the first three words of this quote to be "Some who profess..."

3. Etienne Gilson, *The Spirit of Mediaeval Philosophy* (New York: Charles Scribner's Sons, 1940), 80. Similarly, "In a word, the real object of metaphysics is God." *Christian Philosophy of St. Thomas Aquinas*, 16.

4. Etienne Gilson, "Thomas Aquinas and Our Colleagues," as edited by Anton C. Pegis, *A Gilson Reader* (New York: Doubleday Image Books, 1957), 292.

5. John Wippel, "Teaching Metaphysics: The Value of Aquinas for the Seminarian Today," as edited by Ronald D. Lawler, *Philosophy in Priestly Formation* (Washington: The Catholic University of America, 1978), 116.

6. John M. Quinn, *The Thomism of Etienne Gilson* (Villanova: Villanova University Press, 1971), 4-5.

7. Ibid., 9.

8. Ibid., 13-14.

9. Gilson, *Christian Philosophy of Aquinas*, 16-17.

10. Ibid., 8.

11. Pegis, *A Gilson Reader*, 183.

12. Ibid., 187.

13. Gilson, *Christian Philosophy of Aquinas*, 19. Similarly, Joseph Owens remarks, "Somewhat as the calculations of Adams and Leverrier led to the turning of a telescope on Neptune, so these theological considerations focus attention on the anomaly in the object 'being'." "Aquinas –'Darkness of Ignorance' in the Most Refined Notion of God," *The Southwestern Journal of Philosophy*, 5 (1974), 109.

14. Gilson, *Christian Philosophy of Aquinas*, 22.

15. Maritain crafts this image to characterize Descartes' separation of philosophy from revelation. See Jacques Maritain's *Science and Wisdom* (London: The Centenary Press, 1944), 85.

16. Gilson, *Spirit of Mediaeval Philosophy*, 80. Likewise: "This determination [that God is the real object of metaphysics]. . ., in no way contradicts the one which elsewhere brings him to define metaphysics as the science of being considered simply as being, and of its first causes. If the metaphysician's research deals immediately with being in general, this is not its real end. Philosophical speculation moves beyond being in general towards the first cause of all being." *Christian Philosophy of Aquinas*, 16.

17. "There is one [theology] that treats of divine things, not as the subject of the science but as the principles of its subject [*ens inquantum ens*]. This is the kind of theology pursued by the philosophers and that is also called metaphysics." Thomas Aquinas, *In de Trin.* V, 4c; trans. by Armand Maurer, *The Division and Methods of the Sciences* (Toronto: Pontifical Institute of Mediaeval Studies, 1963), 44. Also, Aquinas, *In Meta.*, proem.

18. Pegis, *A Gilson Reader*, 290-1.

19. Gilson would perhaps utilize only positive judgment to begin metaphysics. See his comments on Maritain in *Christian Philosophy of Aquinas*, 43-44. Gilson sets aside Maritain's "real being in all the purity and amplitude of its own intelligibility

or its own mystery" for a universal concept of being whose
". . . wealth consists, first, of all the judgments of existence
it virtually comprises and connotes." For a discussion of the
need of *separatio* to start Thomistic metaphysics, see my "Immateriality
and Metaphysics," *Angelicum*, 65 (1988), 44-76.

20. Gilson, *Christian Philosophy of Aquinas*, 9-15.

21. "Christian Philosophy is thus both theology and philosophy;
and no contradiction is involved in this." Leonard Kennedy
in his review of Quinn's *Thomism of Gilson*, *The New Scholasticism*,
49 (1975), 370. A distinction can be, and perhaps should be,
made between philosophy as practiced by the theologian and
philosophy as practiced by the philosopher. See Anton Pegis,
The Middle Ages and Philosophy (Chicago: Henry Regnery Company:
1963), ch. 5, "The Ambivalence of Scholasticism."

22. Quinn, op. cit., 3.

23. Ibid., 7.

24. Etienne Gilson, *Elements of Christian Philosophy* (Garden
City, N.Y.: Doubleday & Company, Inc., 1960), 131.

25. Etienne Gilson, *Le Thomisme: Introduction a la Philosophie
de Saint Thomas D'Aquin* (Paris: Librairie Philosophique J. Vrin,
1972), 184. Gilson insists that only judgment can attain esse:
". . . le jugement seul peut atteindre l'existence. . . . l'acte
de juger peut seul atteindre le réel dans sa racine." Ibid.,
185. Incidently, the above quote from 184 enables one to
see that Gilson is unopposed to a conceptualizing of existence.
Once existence is grasped by judgment, the intellect does go
on to conceptualize this object. What Gilson opposes is
conceptualization as the *original* grasp of *esse*. Judgment is
that. For the claim that Gilson is opposed to all conceptualizing
of existence, see Quinn, op. cit., 54-9.

26. "Une métaphysique de l'être en tant qu'être 'consignifie'
l'existence, elle ne la 'signifie' pas, à moins précisément qu'elle

n'use de la deuxième opération de l'entendement et mette en oeuvre toutes les ressources du jugement. Le sentiment, si juste en soi, que le concept universel d'être est le contraire d'une notion vide, trouvera là de quoi se justifier. Sa richesse est d'abord faite de tous les jugements d'existence qu'elle résume et qu'elle connote, . . ." *Le Thomisme.*, 188.

27. Gilson, *Elements.*, 232.

28. "The human intellect thus reaches, even in its most natural operations, a layer of being more deeply seated than essences." Loc. cit.

29. Joseph Owens, *An Interpretation of Existence* (Houston: Center for Thomistic Studies, 1985), 132. In a footnote, Owens' quote refers to *Elements*, 131-33.

30. Gilson, *Elements*, 131.

31. Ibid., 133.

32. Quoted by Gilson, *Elements*, 127.

33. *Elements*, 128.

34. Etienne Gilson, *Being and Some Philosophers* (Toronto: Pontifical Institute of Mediaeval Studies, 1952), 201. Also, "Assuredly, the actual existence of what the terms of a judgment signify is directly or indirectly required for the truth of any predication, but the formal correctness of such a judgment as *all swans are white* is independent of its truth," ibid., 196. "The proper function of judgment is to say existence," ibid., 202.

35. Gilson, *Christian Philosophy of Aquinas*, 41. Also, "All this becomes evident in the case of a judgment of existence, for example: *Socrates is.* Such a proposition clearly expresses by its very composition the composition of the substance Socrates and its existence in reality," loc. cit.

36. ". . . prima operatio respicit quidditatem rei; secunda respicit esse ipsius. Et quia ratio veritatis fundatur in esse, et non in quidditate, ut dictum est, ideo veritas et falsitas proprie invenitur in secunda operatione, et in signo ejus quod est enuntiatio, . . ." *In I Sent.* d. 19, q. 5, a. 1, ad 7m; Mandonnet ed., I, 489.

37. "[Noster intellectus] componit autem aut dividit applicando intelligibilia prius abstracta ad res." *Contra Gentiles* II, 96, *Palam.*

38. *S.T.* I, 86, 1c; *In II Sent.* d. 3, q. 3, ad 1m; *De Ver.* II, 6c.

39. Etienne Gilson, *Thomist Realism and the Critique of Knowledge* (San Francisco: Ignatius Press, 1986), trans. by Mark A. Wauck, 191. See also 205.

40. Ibid., 191.

41. Aquinas speaks of individual generable and corruptible things as *possibilia esse et non esse* at C.G. I, 15, *Amplius* and II, 15, *Praeterea.*

42. For an elaboration of this point, see Knasas, "Immateriality and Metaphysics," 68-74.

GILSON'S USE OF HISTORY IN PHILOSOPHY

Armand A. Maurer, C.S.B.

The perceptive reader of Gilson's philosophical works will quickly realize that they differ in kind. Some are histories of the philosophies of individual men, like Augustine, Bonaventure, Thomas Aquinas, Duns Scotus and Descartes.[1] The purpose of these histories is to present an accurate account of an individual's philosophical views mainly based upon his own writings. The sources of his doctrine, its relation to other philosophies and to contemporary cultural and intellectual movements are not neglected; they serve to throw into sharper focus the individual philosophy under examination. Besides these works Gilson wrote general histories of philosophy, such as the *History of Christian Philosophy in the Middle Ages*[2] and his contributions to *Modern Philosophy*[3] and *Recent Philosophy: Hegel to the Present.*[4] These histories present the philosophical ideas of a group or series of philosophers who lived in a certain historical era or cultural milieu. Though they deal with individual philosophies, emphasis is given to the development of philosophical ideas in history, to the variety of doctrinal currents and their interrelations, the origin of new ideas, their growth and sometimes their neglect and distortion in subsequent schools of philosophy. Gilson the philosopher is always present in these histories, for one cannot engage in the history of philosophy without being a philosopher and revealing, however indirectly, one's own philosophical

commitments.[5]   But here it is not Gilson who philosophizes
but the philosopher or philosophers whom he has chosen as
his subject.

There is a third genre of Gilson's philosophical writings
which is perhaps more typically Gilsonian.   These are not
histories of philosophy at all, though they may appear to be
because they contain so much history of philosophy.   For
this reason they are often read, and sometimes criticized, as
though they were histories of philosophy.   The works to which
I am alluding are not, in Gilson's view, historical but philosophical
in purpose, but they use the history of philosophy in order
to philosophize.   In them the experience of the history of
philosophy is the starting point for philosophical reflection. Some
of Gilson's best known works belong to this category, notably
The Unity of Philosophical Experience[6] and *Being and Some
Philosophers*.[7]   Beyond the history of philosophy, these books
aim to give a philosophical explanation of the history of philosophy,
and that, according to Gilson, is the task of philosophy itself.[8]

The philosophical character of *Being and Some Philosophers*
is clear from the Preface. Gilson writes:

> [T]his is not a book in the history of philosophy;
> it is a philosophical book, and a dogmatically
> philosophical one at that....as a history, this
> book would be entirely wrong. The choice
> of the philosophers singled out for special
> consideration, the selection the theses to be
> discussed within their own particular
> philosophies, the intentional disregarding of
> all unnecessary display of historical erudition,
> everything in it is bound to appear as historical
> arbitrariness; and this is just what it is, since
> each and every line of this book is philosophic,
> if not in its form, at least in its purpose.
> Its author may well have committed historical
> mistakes; he has not committed the deadly

> one of mistaking philosophy for history. For
> the only task of history is to understand
> and to make understood, whereas philosophy
> must choose; and applying to history for
> reasons to make a choice is no longer history,
> it is philosophy.[9]

The Unity of Philosophical Experience belongs to the same
philosophical genre. From three historical "experiments"—medieval,
Cartesian and modern—Gilson draws intelligible laws which
in his estimation transcend history and belong to philosophy
itself.   His historical method of philosophizing in this work
resembles that of William James's *The Varieties of Religious
Experience*,[10] which moves from the description of a vast collection
of recorded religious experiences to general conclusions—with
at least the value of probability—that belong to the philosophy
of religion.

What is the nature of the method Gilson uses in this
category of his philosophical works?   What justification can
be given for the method?   What are its strengths and weaknesses?
And what is the value of the conclusions reached?   Answers
to some of these questions are broached in *The Unity of Philosophical
Experience* and *Being and Some Philosophers*, but Gilson's
most direct and explicit account of his method is found in
his important address "Remarques sur l'expérience en métaphysique,"
given at Brussels in 1953 to the Eleventh International Congress
of Philosophy.[11]   Because the address deserves to be better
known in English-speaking circles, a translation of it is appended
to this study.

Philosophizing in the tradition of Aristotle and Thomas
Aquinas, Gilson's starting point could only be experience. Though
he was not trained as an historian in the strict sense,[12] his
courses at the Lycée Henri IV and the Sorbonne, and his
own subsequent researches, gave him a wealth of experience
in the history of philosophy on which to reflect philosophically.
A philosopher philosophizes from the experience at his command.

In Gilson's case it was the experience of the history of philosophy. What he needed was a method for a philosophical reflection on that history. He conceived that method as a kind of experimentation on the philosophical—and especially the metaphysical—data furnished by history.

The notion of a philosopher experimenting with anything is bound to seem a bit odd, if not downright absurd. Experimentation is an essential part of the method of science; at first sight it does not appear to have a place in philosophy. We generally think of an experiment as the manipulation of sensible phenomena resulting in an observation that will either verify or falsify an hypothesis. In the language of Claude Bernard (whom Gilson cites in this connection), an experiment is an "induced observation" (*observation provoquée*), that is to say, an experience of a fact brought to light through the action of an experimenter upon nature. Other observations called upon to prove or disprove an hypothesis are simply "invoked" (*invoquées*), that is, they are appealed to as experiences of facts presenting themselves spontaneously and naturally, without the investigator's altering the circumstances or conditions in which they reveal themselves. As for experience itself, Gilson follows Bernard in defining it as "every observation that is either induced or invoked in order to verify an hypothesis, that is, to prove it true or false."[4][13]

Gilson was under no illusion that a philosopher, using the data of history, could perform experiments so as to produce new observations in order to verify or falsify a philosophical hypothesis. This would entail his acting upon the past, which is a patent absurdity. Gilson leaves open the possibility of causing a metaphysical experience in the present, say in a philosophical discussion. What is certain is that a philosopher can observe the history of philosophy and assure himself that certain conclusions necessarily flow from a principle by seeing them in fact come from it. He can ask: What happens if *x* is laid down as a principle? Experience will help him to give the answer. By calling on the data of history he can see what consequences have in fact emerged from it; and if he cannot accept the consequences he must abandon the principle. [4]

For Gilson this procedure is rightly called an experiment, though not in the sense in which the word is used in the physical sciences. It is not an experiment performed in a laboratory but in the mind; it does not have to do with things but with ideas. It is the general opinion, Gilson remarks, that sensible phenomena alone are resistant enough to be experimented upon, but this is an illusion. "Abstract ideas," he continues, "have a resistance and, so to speak, a solidity of their own. The slightest alteration in their comprehension never fails to bring about a corresponding alteration in the whole series of their consequences."[14]

This important fact makes it possible to engage in experiments with the data of the history of philosophy, such as Gilson carries out, for example, in *Being and Some Philosophers*. His experimentation in this book begins—as he insists all philosophical experiments do—with an hypothesis. Suppose being is conceived as "existentially neutral," that is to say, by dismissing actual existence from the content of the notion. Suppose, further, that we agree with Parmenides in carrying this notion of being to its absolutely ultimate conclusions. We can then say that being is; we cannot say that it is not. And since being has no admixture of non-being, it admits of no otherness, but is perfectly self-identical, absolutely one and unchanging. Then the world of existence given to us in sensible experience, which is subject to change and diversity, is not being but rather an appearance or illusion.[15] Gilson follows the long history of western metaphysics, from the Greeks to modern existentialists for whom existence is a lack or disease of being, showing that a notion of being without actual existence always leads to unacceptable conclusions, as do all attempts to replace being as the primary notion with one of its many possible surrogates, such as form, substance or essence. Thomas Aquinas, in his view, offers the only acceptable choice for the philosopher by positing the act of existing at the core of the notion of being and reality.

Another example of a Gilsonian philosophical experiment, chosen from among many in *The Unity of Philosophical Experience*, concerns the possibility of an intuitive knowledge of something that does not exist and the consequent tendency of skepticism in philosophy. From the theological principle of the omnipotence of God, Ockham concludes that God can always do by himself what he normally does through secondary causes. When we look at a star in the sky, our perception is normally caused by God as the primary cause and by the star as a secondary cause. However, since God can always produce one absolute thing without another, he can give us the sight of the star without the existence of the star.[16] Following this line of thought, nothing can assure us of the reality of the sensible world, and we end up with the idealism of Berkeley: nothing is necessarily required to make knowledge possible except the mind and God.[17]

Experiences of this sort help us to see how Gilson envisages the history of philosophy as a basis of philosophical reflection. We can observe the principles laid down by philosophers, and we can see how, over a period of time (which may be centuries) subsequent philosophers draw from the principles their possible consequences, even those unforeseen by the masters themselves. We can then construct from these historical data abstract sequences of ideas which are in themselves independent of time. Time was needed for their development, but the sequences of ideas themselves abstract from time and history. In Gilson's words, the philosopher can "step outside of time" and consider a sequence of ideas for its own sake, concentrating on the permanent necessity of the contents of the ideas, abstracting from the contingent and transitory historical conditions of its formation. In this perspective the sequence of ideas initiated by a philosopher can no longer be given his name, for he is not responsible for the subsequent development of the ideas. "No philosopher in particular," Gilson writes, "is responsible for the sequence even if he originates it. Aristotle is not responsible for Averroes, nor for St. Thomas Aquinas, nor for William of Ockham. The names that can be cited in such cases are only signs of the historical stages illustrating the successive moments of a sequence that never existed in the mind of any philosopher."[3]

In proposing an abstract construction of sequences of ideas from the data of the history of philosophy, Gilson does not intend to reduce the philosophers themselves to these ideas. When the philosopher uses the history of individual philosophies in order to philosophize, he must leave out of account many elements of the philosophies that belong to them by right and that should enter into the historian's perspective.   Gilson makes this abundantly clear in the conclusion of *The Unity of Philosophical Experience*:

> [I]n order to stress certain sequences of ideas, and to make clear their ideological articulations, we had to detach them from the philosophical organisms whose parts they were. This, of course, is always detrimental to such organisms, and highly objectionable from the point of view of the philosophers themselves. A philosophical doctrine is not defined merely by its general spirit, its fundamental principles, and the consequences to which they actually lead its author. It is made up of many other elements which enter its structure and share in determining its concrete individual nature. What a philosopher has not seen in his own principles, even though it may flow from them with absolute necessity, does not belong to *his* philosophy. The possible consequences which the philosopher has seen, but which he has tried to evade, and has finally disavowed, should not be ascribed to him, even though he should have held them on the strength of his own principles;

they are no part of his philosophy. On
the other side, all those subtle shades of
thoughts which qualify the principles of a
philosopher soften their rigidity and allow
them to do justice to the complexity of
concrete facts, are not only part and parcel
of his own doctrine, but are often the only
part of it that will survive the death of
the system.[18]

This should put us on guard against reading as histories
of philosophies the works of Gilson in which he philosophizes
on the data of the history of philosophy. In these works
his aim is not to give an account of a particular philosophy
as it existed in the mind of its author. Rather, Gilson abstracts
from a philosophy one of its leading principles and constructs
a sequence of ideas that necessarily flow from the principle
either in that particular philosophy or in subsequent philosophies.
In so doing he leaves aside, or gives little attention to other
principles in the philosophy that limit and modify the consequences
of the first principle.

Gilson learned from Victor Delbos, one of his Sorbonne
professors, that "every philosophical doctrine is the result not
of one principle but of a compromise among a number of
principles, some of which serve to prevent any one of the
others from developing the whole train of its consequences."[1]
As early as 1925 he said in an interview:

[T]he actual philosophy of a Descartes, a
St. Thomas or a St. Bonaventure is always
a system of theses in which each thesis,
taken in isolation, would destroy the equilibrium
of the doctrine if the thesis were left to
develop on its own account. The work
of the philosopher is precisely to ensure
that equilibrium by adjusting and organizing
the theses.[19]

In his Brussels lecture Gilson illustrates this observation
by the philosophy of Descartes.   The starting point of the
Cartesian system is the method of clear and distinct ideas,
which allows a philosopher to assent only to clearly and distinctly
perceived objects of thought. Following this method, Descartes
separated thought from extension, for each has its own clear
and distinct idea.   An immediate consequence is the real distinction between mind and body. And yet Descartes was convinced
from experience that the mind and body form a substantial
unity (*unité par soi*)[20]—a fact difficult to reconcile with the
consequences of the method of clear and distinct ideas.   Descartes
brought the two theses together in his doctrinal synthesis, but
the tension this created in the system prompted successors like
Malebranche, Leibniz and Spinoza to look for other ways of
conceiving the relation between mind and body.   The Cartesian
school followed the normal pattern of upsetting the master's
doctrinal synthesis by favoring one of his principles at the
expense of the others.   Descartes himself had limited the consequences of his method in order to make room for the real
unity of the human person.   His followers upset the balance
of the system by refusing to restrict the consequences of the
method out of regard for that unity.[2]

Gilson could just as well have cited the doctrinal synthesis
of William of Ockham to illustrate his point.   As we have
seen, from the principle of the divine omnipotence Oakham
concluded that God could give us an intuition of something
that does not exist. If this is the case, Gilson the philosopher
asks:

> How shall we ever be sure that what we
> are perceiving as real is an actually existing
> thing?   In other words, if it is possible
> for God to make us perceive as real an
> object that does not really exist, have we
> any proof that this world of ours is not
> a vast phantasmagoria behind which there
> is no reality to be found?[21]

But Gilson the historian of philosophy knows well that
Ockham himself never came to this conclusion, for there is
another principle in Ockhamism that holds the conclusion in
check, namely that evident knowledge requires the existence
of its object. For Ockham, the intuitive knowledge of existing
things is the perfect type of evident knowledge. Hence, if
we have an evident intuition of something, that thing must
exist. In the event of God's creating in us an intuition of
a non-existent object, we would evidently judge that the thing
does not exist.[22]   Indeed, Ockham grants that the intuition
of a non-existent object, supernaturally created in us by God,
would not, for lack of evidence, be truly intuitive but abstractive
knowledge.[23]   By thus holding in check the full consequences
of the principle of divine omnipotence by the principle of
evident knowledge, Ockham does not avoid all philosophical
difficulties; but he creates a balance in his philosophy that
saves it from skepticism regarding the reality of the external
world. Skepticism entered into late medieval philosophy when
the equilibrium of Ockham's philosophy was upset by emphasizing
the omnipotence of God and removing the principle of evident
knowledge. Reflecting on experiences of this sort, Gilson formulates
the general law: "Each principle a philosopher sets in motion
tends to develop for its own sake among his followers and
to yield spontaneously the train of its consequence."[2]

What is the role of this experimental method in metaphysics and what value does it have? Gilson sees the method
as purely dialectical and its conclusions only probable. The
fact that certain conclusions necessarily follow from a principle
does not prove that the conclusions are necessary in themselves
or that the principle from which they flow is true or false.
History only guarantees that the conclusions have necessarily
emerged from the principle, and it is then up to the philosopher
to see the truth. If he cannot accept the conclusions because
they are not in accord with reality, he must give up the principle;
and if for the same reason he cannot accept the principle,
he must deny the conclusions. Thus the dialectic of history
can help him to arrive at the truth, but it cannot give it
to him.[6]

Because of its dialectical character Gilson denies that the experimental method he has described can be the proper method of metaphysics. Metaphysics as a science does not rest on the experience of the history of philosophy but on the intellectual intuition of principles and the direct perception of their truth.[5] Gilson here remains faithful to Thomas Aquinas, who describes the proper mode of knowing in metaphysics as *intellectus*, which is an act of intellectual insight.[24] Knowledge gained through *intellectus* has its origin in the senses and it is not mediated by any previous intellectual knowledge. In other words, it is not a conclusion drawn from principles but the immediate grasping of principles themselves, and especially being, which is the absolutely first principle. The intuition of principles is also necessary and not probable knowledge, for it cannot be otherwise. Broadening the term "experience" as Claude Bernard used it, Gilson suggests that this intellectual intuition may be called "metaphysical experience," and he offers it as the only direct access to the truths of metaphysics.[5][25]

If metaphysics has its own method, why should the metaphysician resort to experimentation in the history of philosophy? Gilson sees this need because the intellectual intuition of principles is so difficult and insecure. The metaphysician needs auxiliary methods in order to gain the intuition, to deepen it, and to maintain it. Though experience in the history of philosophy is not metaphysical experience itself, but only a secondary and supportive method for arriving at it, "it helps us to discover [the truth] by circumscribing the areas in which truth is found, by helping us to recognize it, and by protecting the mind from the risks of losing it."[7] In Gilson's terse formula: "It does not make us see; it leads us to the point from where we see."[9]

Jacques Maritain also acknowledges the value of concrete approaches which prepare for the intuition of being and lead up to it. Among these approaches he mentions Bergson's experience of duration, Heidegger's experience of anguish, and Marcel's experience of moral virtues such as fidelity. Maritain sees

value in these experiences for directing the metaphysician to
the intuition of being, though he does not think they give
him that intuition. They bring one to the threshold of metaphysics,
he claims, but then it is up to the metaphysician to take
the decisive step and cross over into metaphysics proper.[26] Though
Gilson does not see eye to eye with Maritain on the nature
of the intuition of being,[27] he agrees with him on the importance
of concrete paths to it.   Gilson's own contribution to these
paths is experience in the history of philosophy: a humble
path indeed, but yielding precious fruits in his philosophical
works.[28]

Pontifical Institute of Mediaeval Studies
Toronto, Ontario

NOTES

1. *The Christian Philosophy of St. Augustine*, trans. L. E. Lynch (New York: Random House, 1960); *The Philosophy of St. Bonaventure*, trans. Dom I. Trethowan & F. J. Sheed (New York: Sheed and Ward, 1938; *The Christian Philosophy of St. Thomas Aquinas*, trans. L. K. Shook (New York: Random House, 1956); *La liberté chez Descartes et la théologie* (Paris: F. Alcan, 1913); *Jean Duns Scot: Introduction à ses positions fondamentales* (Paris: J. Vrin, 1952). For the writings of Etienne Gilson, see M. McGrath, *Etienne Gilson, A Bibliography* (Toronto: Pontifical Institute of Mediaeval Studies, 1982).

2. (New York: Random House, 1955).

3. (New York: Random House, 1963).

4. (New York: Random House, 1966).

5. "No man can write a single line of history of philosophy without handling his subject as a philosopher." E. Gilson, "Doctrinal History and its Interpretation," *Speculum* 24 (1949), 489.

6. (New York: Scribner's, 1937).

7. 2nd ed. (Toronto: Pontifical Institute of Mediaeval Studies, 1952). Other philosophical works of Gilson in which he uses history are: *Reason and Revelation in the Middle Ages* (New York: Scribner's, 1938); *God and Philosophy* (New York: Yale University Press, 1941); *Réalisme thomiste et critique de la connaissance* (Paris: J. Vrin, 1947) *Thomist Realism and the Critique of Knowledge*, trans. M. A. Wauck (San Francisco: Ignatius Press, 1986).

8. *The Unity of Philosophical Experience*, 304. For Gilson's views on the relation of philosophy to history see his article, "Le rôle de la philosophie dans l'histoire de la civilisation," *Proceedings of the Sixth International Congress of Philosophy*, Harvard, 1926 (New York & London, 1927), 529-535. On this subject see H. Gouhier, "De l'histoire à la philosophie, "*Etienne Gilson, philosophe de la chrétienté* (Paris, 1949), 53-

69 and A. Livi, "Etienne Gilson: metafisica e metodologia dell'esperienza storica," *Filosofia oggi* 7 (1984), 547-556.

9. *Being and Some Philosophers*, ix-x. In *The Spirit of Mediaeval Philosophy*, trans. A. H. C. Downes (New York: Scribner's, 1940), Gilson uses the history of philosophy to show that the Middle Ages produced a specifically Christian philosophy. See Preface, vii.

10. (New York: Longmans, 1902).

11. See below, Appendix, note 1.

12. "Gilson n'avait pas de dormation technique d'historien, mais sa curiosité d'esprit et son goût des réalités le disposaient à apprecier l'importance des documents." Marie-Thérèse d'Alverny, "Nécrologie. Etienne Gilson (1884-1978)," *Cahiers de civilisation medieval* 22 (1979), 426. For Gilson's life and works, see L. K. Shook, *Etienne Gilson* (Toronto: Pontifical Institute of Mediaeval Studies, 1985).

13. References in square brackets are to the paragraphs of Gilson's address translated and printed at the end of this paper. Gilson refers to Claude Bernard's *An Introduction to the Study of Experimental Medicine*, trans. H. C. Greene (New York: Dover Publications, 1959), 19-20.

14. *Being and Some Philosophers*, 6.

15. Ibid., 9.

16. Ockham, *Scriptum in librum primum Sententiarum*, Prol., q. 1; d. G. Gal, S. Brown. *Opera theologica* I (St. Bonaventure, New York: Franciscan Institute, 1967), 38.15-39.6.

17. *The Unity of Philosophical Experience*, 81-82.

18. Ibid., 300-301.

19. F. Lefèvre, *Une heure avec Etienne Gilson* (Paris: Gallimard,

1925), 71. "Each particular philosophy is . . . a co-ordination of self and mutually limiting principles which defines an individual outlook on the fullness of reality." E. Gilson, *The Unity of Philosophical Experience*, 301.

20. See below, Appendix, note 2.

21. Ibid., 80-81.

22. Ockham, ibid., 31.11-16. See Gilson, ibid., 80. Gilson's pages on Ockham's doctrine of intuition of non-existents in *The Unity of Philosophical Experience* have often been misread and criticized as though he intended to write a history of Ockham's philosophy. In fact, his approach to Ockham is philosophical, using the history of philosophy. These pages are understandable against the background of his method described in the Brussels address.

23. Ockham, *Quodlibet* V, q. 5. *Quodlibeta septem*, ed. J. C. Wey. *Opera theologica* IX (St. Bonaventure, N.Y., 1980), 498.61-76.

24. St. Thomas, *Expositio super librum Boethii De Trinitate*, VI, 1; ed. B. Decker (Leiden: E. J. Brill, 1955), 210.29-212.25. Trans. A. Maurer, *Thomas Aquinas. The Division and Methods of the Sciences*, 4th ed. (Toronto: Pontifical Institute of Mediaeval Studies, 1986), 70-73.

25. The term *expérience métaphysique* is also used by J. Maritain in *Les degrés du savior* (Paris: Desclée, 1932), 551.

26. J. Maritain, *A Preface to Metaphysics* (London: Sheed & Ward, 1943), 49-52.

27. The subject is too complex to be dealt with here. Gilson explains his disagreement with Maritain in *Le thomisme*, 6th ed. (Paris: J. Vrin, 1965), 187-188 (*The Christian Philosophy of St. Thomas Aquinas*, 43-44), especially in one of his final articles "Propos sur l'être et sa notion," *San Tommaso e il pensiero moderno: saggi. Studi Thomistici* 3. Pontifica Accademia

Romana di S. Tommaso d'Aquino (Rome, Citta Nuova Editrice, 1974), 7-17, replying to Maritain's "Reflexions sur la nature blessee et sur l'intuition de l'être," *Revue thomiste* 68 (1968), 17-34. (Reprinted in J. Maritain, *Approches san entraves* [Paris: Fayard, 1973], 264-284). In brief, Gilson denies, in opposition to Maritain, that we can have an intellectual intuition of the act of existing (*esse*) of a being. We perceive that act of existing only in sensible perception of the substance that it actualizes. Neither do we have a concept of the act of existing distinct from that of the being whose act it is. See E. Gilson, "Propos sur l'etre et sa notion," 10. "Sensible data are directly known as beings, so that an intuitive experience of their acts of existing is included in the intellectual knowledge we have of them." E. Gilson, *L'être et l'essence*, 2nd ed. (Paris, 1962), 299.

28. John M. Quinn misconstrues Gilson's historical method in his *The Thomism of Etienne Gilson: A Critical Study* (Villanova University Press, 1971), 23-29. As we have seen, Gilson's use of the term "experiment" does not assimilate "the mode of historical inquiry to the procedures of natural science", 23. By "experiment" Gilson does not mean "the corpus of conclusions comprising the world view of each [philosophical system]", 24. Aristotle's history of philosophical ideas in *Metaphysics* I is not "markedly distinct from that of Gilson's because Aristotle's "forms part of a dialectical prelude to the determination of metaphysical truth", 28. That is exactly what Gilson intends his reflections on the history of philosophy to be.

APPENDIX
REMARKS ON EXPERIENCE IN METAPHYSICS[1]

Etienne Gilson

[1] Victor Delbos[2] used to say that every philosophical doctrine is the result not of one principle but of a compromise among a number of principles, some of which serve to prevent

any one of the others from developing the whole train of its consequences. He knew Kant too well not to have noticed this fact. Even Spinoza, despite his seeming to follow entirely one line of thought, would be another example; and I confess that I have not seen any major philosophy which could not be cited in confirmation of this fact. The proper object of the history of philosophies is precisely the study of these doctrinal equilibriums as they existed in the minds of their authors.

[2] It is difficult, moreover, to cultivate the history of philosophies for long without noticing another fact. Limiting the consequence of one principle by means of another principle does not eliminate the necessity inherent in each principle to develop freely the totality of its possible consequences. From this point of view there is scarcely a doctrinal synthesis that is not the setting for one or more internal conflicts so well known to historians. To mention only one famous example: Descartes always maintained the substantial unity of the human being, composed of a soul and a body;[3] but there is a question of knowing whether it was possible to reach that conclusion starting from the method of clear and distinct ideas, which naturally led to separating thought from extension. Wherever it is found, this second fact gives rise to a third, namely "the school." A school is a group of philosophers who, at the risk of destroying the original equilibrium, succumb to the temptation of showing favor to one of the master's principles at the expense of the others. The occasionalism of Malebranche, the pre-established harmony of Leibniz, the parallelism of Spinoza, are so many possible responses to the problem created by the Cartesian method of clear and distinct ideas. Descartes' reply to Regius's manifesto[4] makes it clear enough that he would not have recognized his own thought in these doctrines. They are not in any sense his own doctrine. It could not even be said that strictly speaking they flow from it. Nevertheless these doctrines, or ones similar to them, followed necessarily from his own as soon as his followers refused to restrict the consequences of the method out of regard for the real unity of the human being. The history of Platonism, Aristotelianism, Kantianism, or Comtism, would suggest a similar conclusion.

Each principle a philosopher sets in motion tends to develop
on its own among his followers and to yield spontaneously
the train of its consequences.

[3] Seen from this point of view, the history of philosophies
presents itself, at least in part, as the development in time
of dialectical sequences which are rightly independent of time.
Because the intellect thinks in time, as Aristotle remarks,[5] it
was necessary that different men, living in different times and
places, bring   the dialectical series flowing from principles
to their respective conclusions.   It nevertheless seems that by
right a non-temporal observer should have been able to predict,
in an *a priori* sort of way, the development of these consequences.
As a matter of fact, if he gives his attention to any one
at all of these doctrinal sequences, the observer steps outside
of history on two scores.   First, because he steps outside
of time.   From this viewpoint the fact that time was needed
for this development to be possible affects neither its meaning
nor its structure.   The duration empirically necessary for their
elaboration is not inscribed in the content of these sequences.
Second, because the observer loses the right to attach proper
names to them.   No particular philosopher is responsible for
the sequence even if he originates it.   Aristotle is not responsible
for Averroes, nor for St. Thomas Aquinas, nor for William
of Ockham.   The names that can be cited in such cases are
only signs of the historical stages illustrating the successive
moments of a sequence that never existed in the mind of
any philosopher.   Each proper name denotes, not the whole
structure nor the particular equilibrium of the doctrine to which
the name is attached, but the particular element which makes
it representative of one of the successive moments of a certain
dialectical sequence.   We can observe this concretely and grasp
it in its living reality in notions like the Idea in Plato, substance
in Aristotle, essence in Avicenna, or the act of existing in
Thomas Aquinas.   But these principles are not tied to any
one man, as is evident from the fact that none of those who
discovered them thought out in advance all their possible consequences.
We leave history therefore and enter into a philosophical reflection
on history.   Though arbitrary from an historical point of view,

this reflection justifies the choice it makes of certain historical materials by the very nature of the abstract sequence it proposes to construct.

[4] It is under this warrant that one can consider such a method as a kind of experimentation on the metaphysical data furnished by history. Claude Bernard called "experiment" every observation that is either induced or invoked in order to verify an hypothesis, that is, of course, with a view to proving it true or false.[6] It would be another problem to know whether we can induce metaphysical experiments in the present, for instance in a philosophical discussion. In any case, it remains certain that, being unable to act on the past, we could not induce anything at all in order to verify any philosophical hypothesis. But we can observe the history of philosophy and appeal to observations with a view to assuring ourselves, by seeing them emerge in fact from a principle, that certain knowledge is in fact contained in it. Then the proof that x by right implies a, b, c, d is that in fact, in the course of time, and sometimes after an interval of centuries, a, b, c, d have finally emerged from it. *Coactus a veritate*, so to speak, an intellect has seen that a certain consequence necessarily followed from a principle, and that we must give up the principle if we cannot accept the consequence, or vice versa. To the abstract question: what happens if we posit x as a principle? The experiment facilitates the answer. By calling upon the data of history we can see concretely what in fact has happened.

[5] What are the nature and scope of such a method? Its nature is indirect, and its immediate scope does not go beyond the level of simple dialectic. This is clear from the fact that the questions whose answers it is looking for all begin with *if*. In other words, we could not make it the method of metaphysics itself. As a science, metaphysics rests on the intellectual intuition of principles and the direct perception of their truth. This immediate knowledge can be called "experience", and, if we agree to call it by this name, it is metaphysical experience. As such, it is necessary, and it alone gives us

direct access to the truth. The experimentation on metaphysics of which we are speaking can only constitute an auxiliary, secondary, and in some way supportive method for metaphysical research properly so called; so it could not under any circumstances replace it.

[6] The reason for its radical inadequacy is its dialectical character, which prevents it from reaching the truth. The fact that certain conclusions follow of necessity from a principle proves neither that these conclusions are necessary in themselves nor that the principle from which they necessarily flow is itself true or false. If we drew up an ideal list of all the series of metaphysical ideas that are dialectically necessary, like the *Summa dialectica* that Mortimer Adler has conceived and is preparing to publish,[7] it would still not be a *Summa philosophica*, because the knowledge of all possible dialectical sequences of ideas would entail neither the truth nor the falsity of any one of them. The same holds for experimentation in the history of philosophies. Leading in every case to an intellectual choice, like that of the mathematician among several equations, it (experimentation) leaves to the philosopher the discernment of the truth, the vision of which will of necessity determine his choice. The only dialectical sequences of ideas that are true and which we must consequently choose, are those that necessarily follow from true principles, and above all from the truth of the first principle. It is not within the capacity of dialectic to give us the intuition of truth.

[7] This does not mean that a method of this sort is philosophically sterile. Though incapable of giving us the truth, it helps us to discover it by circumscribing the areas where truth is found, by helping us to recognize it, and by protecting the understanding from the risks of losing it. I would point out, first of all, that if research of this sort cannot lead to a *Summa philosophica*, nevertheless it would not result in a simple *Summa logica*. Dialectic ceases to be a logic pure and simple to the extent that, in the course of developing the necessary implications of concepts, it subordinates its formalism to their content. In this connection we recall the great dialectic

whose model Plato has left in his dialogues, perhaps above all in the *Sophist* and *Parmenides*. Here it is truly a matter of Ideas—I would almost say of "mother-ideas"—whose content dominates and determines the mind that puts them to the test. The formal necessity of the dialectic is tied up with the real necessity of essences and their concepts.

[8] That is not all, for although metaphysical truth depends on the evidence of principles directly perceived, and on it alone, it is not easy or even inevitable that we reach these principles. Every human intellect necessarily knows the first principles, but it does not necessarily know that it knows them, nor that they are principles. Moreover, even if it distinctly knows the first principle as a principle, the intellect that sees the evidence for it does not necessarily exhaust its content. Aristotle, Thomas Aquinas, Duns Scotus, Ockham, and still others whom it would be easy to name, agree that being is the first principle, but they give different answers to the question: what is being? This is so true that even within philosophical schools we observe the paradoxical fact that the disciples do not always understand the first principle in the same sense as the master whom they claim as their own. We can close our eyes to this fact but we cannot make it go away, for it is true even within a school as traditionally united as that of the Thomists. Banez, whose testimony on this point is difficult to deny, took note of it as firmly as possible: "Et hoc est quod saepissime D. Thomas clamat, et Thomistae nolunt audire: quod esse est actualitas omnis formae vel naturae . . ." (*Comm. in* I, q. 3, a. 4).8 The history of doctrine fully confirms this remark. There have not been wanting "Thomists" who, though placed in the presence of the first principle of St. Thomas and informed by him as to its meaning, have remained incapable of seeing that meaning. And what truth can one see clearly if one does not see clearly the truth of the first principle?

[9] Here again the observation of the history of doctrines, deliberately called to witness, can take on the value of an experiment in metaphysics. Although it does not make us

see, it puts us on the path of the principles and it clarifies
their meaning by bringing to light the train of their necessary
consequences. For indeed, if metaphysics is a real science
and not a simple dialectic, its conclusions in the final analysis
are justifiable by their agreement with reality. The metaphysics
of being that can with certainty be said to be true is that
which conceives being such as it is. Between two possible
metaphysics our intellect ought to reserve its assent for the
one that recognizes all that being is and posits it such as
it is, but ought to refuse its assent for the one that does
not see all that it is and as a consequence leads us to describe
it such as it is not. It is here, and on this specific level,
that in its own way experimentation in matters of the history
of doctrines appears irreplaceable. It helps us to recognize
true principles and to discern their meaning by seeing their
necessary consequences. It does not make us see; it leads
us to the point from where we see. Finally, it avoids being
content with one of these superficial views of principles that
permits the use of words emptied of part of their meaning—
too often the most profound part—and perpetuates misunderstandings
among philosophers, best qualified to understand each other.
Although it is entirely secondary, this kind of service is not
to be disdained.

[10] The question remains why the construction of these
dialectical sequences of ideas requires the use of history. We
have already suggested that there is here no theoretical necessity,
but there is a practical necessity. By right a single mind
ought to be able to deduce *a priori* all the sequences of
principles and conclusions accessible to reason. In fact, philosophy
does not proceed in this way. Many philosophers, and sometimes
many centuries, are needed for the understanding to uncover
the deep meaning and the main implications of a principle.
The Hegelian dialectic of the history of philosophy presupposes
that history. It prophesies in the past: it makes us see so
clearly with what consequences the being of Parmenides was
pregnant only because these consequences have already emerged
from it. Parmenides himself could not have foreseen them.
Moreover, that is also why Hegel, placing himself hypothetically
in the situation of a superhuman intellect which by itself would

dispense with all the others, had to construct a dialectic of history instead of observing its real dialectics, such as they offer themselves to the eyes of the philosopher who pays attention to the analyses of the historian.   There is no skepticism or relativism here.   Devotion to the truth should not exclude modesty, and the demands of the human condition weigh equally upon all men, even upon the minds of metaphysicians.

NOTES FOR APPENDIX

1. Etienne Gilson, "Remarques sur l'expérience en métaphysique," *Actes du XIe Congrès international de philosophie*, Brussels, August 20-26, 1953, vol. 4 (Amsterdam: North-Holland, 1953), 5-10.   Paragraphs have been numbered and notes added by the translator.   I am grateful to Cecile Gilson for permission to publish a translation of the article.

2.   One of Gilson's philosophy teachers at the Sorbonne. Gilson writes about him in *The Philosopher and Theology*.

3.   In a letter to Regius, Descartes says that the soul and body are composed *per veram unionem substantialem. Vie et oeuvres de Descartes*, ed. Adam-Tannery, vol. 3 (Paris: Cerf, 1899), 508.36.   See ibid.,   493.3-5.   Regius (d. 1679) was professor of medicine and botany at the University of Utrecht. See Paul Hoffman, "The Unity of Descartes's Man," *The Philosophical Review* 95 (1986), 339-370.

4.   Having been a disciple of Descartes, Regius turned against him and published a sort of Program in which he maintained positions opposed to those of his former master. See *Vie et oeuvres de Descartes*, supplément à l'édition de Descartes, ed. Adam-Tannery, vol. 12, 351.   Regius's *Programma* is edited in vol. 8, 2² partie, 342-346.   Descartes replied to Regius in *Notae in Programma*, ibid., 346-369.

5.   Perhaps Gilson alludes to Aristotle's statement that time is a good discoverer and partner in the pursuit of the truth. See Aristotle, *Nicomachean Ethics* I, 7 (1098a23).

6.   Gilson refers to Bernard's distinction between an "induced observation" (*observation provoquée*) and one that is simply "invoked" (*invoquée*).   In the latter case the observed fact is noted without having to make it appear or to produce it. See Claude Bernard, *An Introduction to the Study of Experimental Medicine*, trans. H. C. Greene (New York: Dover Publications, 1957), 9-20.

7.   Adler did not publish his proposed *Summa dialectica*. He has, however, produced a dialectical study of the notion of freedom: *The Idea of Freedom. A Dialectical Examination of the Conceptions of Freedom* (Garden City, New York: Doubleday, 1958).

8.   "And this is what St. Thomas very often proclaimed and Thomists will not hear, that *esse* is the actuality of every form or nature." Domingo Bañez, O.P., *Scholastica commentaria in primam partem Summae Theologiae S. Thomae Aquinatis*, I, 3, a. 4; ed. Luis Urbano (Madrid: Editorial F.E.D.A., 1934), I, 141a.   Gilson frequently refers to Bañez' saying.   See for example, "Trois leçons sur le Thomisme et sa situation présente," *Seminarium* 17 (1965), 693.

THOMISM AND DIVINE
ABSOLUTE POWER

Leonard A. Kennedy, C.S.B.

One of the most common features of philosophy and theology between the death of St. Thomas Aquinas and the Protestant Reformation was a certain interpretation of divine power. We shall see to what extent this interpretation existed in the three major schools of this period: the Scotist, Ockhamist, and Thomist. It cannot be found at all in the Averroist school, which did not admit in philosophy the existence of a creating God. Nor can it be found in the Platonist school, which arose at the end of the period we are considering; this school had its own specialized concerns.

Writers of the schools we shall be examining agreed that God is of infinite power and that, as a matter of fact, He has not used all this power in the realm of creation. The power which God *has* used is called His ordinate power (*potentia ordinata*), that is, the power manifested in the natural and supernatural orders He has established. All agreed also that God could still exercise hitherto unused power in accordance with these orders, and that this would still be His ordinate power; for example, if he performed new miracles. And all agreed that the excess of power left to God, by which He could establish a new order if He wished, is His absolute power (*potentia absoluta*). God could, for example, have established a physical order different from the present one, indeed incompatible with it, with different laws.

What the writers disagreed on was the *content* of this absolute power. To put it another way: they agreed that it is limited only by the principle of non-contradiction, but they disagreed on what constitutes a contradiction. This power is called absolute because it is the divine power considered without relationship to the divine wisdom or goodness. The devotees of the doctrine of divine absolute power (let us call them henceforth the divine power philosophers) said that God could do whatever is not a contradiction, taking into account only His power. Those opposed to them said that the notion of divine absolute power is a useless notion, a non-applicable one, since it is a contradiction for God to do what is against His wisdom or goodness.

Medieval writers agreed that God's absolute power, by definition, includes the ability to do what is against the divine wisdom or goodness. But those who refused to use the notion added that such an ability is not a real ability; that, in fact, it is a contradiction for God to act against His wisdom or goodness. The divine power philosophers contended, on the other hand, at least implicitly, that God, by His absolute power, could actually act against His wisdom or goodness. They didn't put it this way; what they said was that God could do whatever is not a contradiction, but the *examples* they gave show that they thought that God could do what is against His wisdom and goodness.

What we are studying is a philosophical problem: the role of secondary causality in a creationist metaphysics. If God is the first cause of the existence and the operation of each creature, what necessity can be found in the created universe? Is the contingency of this universe total? Granted that creatures need not have been, what necessity accrues to them once they do exist? The divine power philosophers tended to remove all necessity from creaturely existence and operation, some of these philosophers going much further than others.

Their motive in doing so was to give glory to God by stressing His power. They thought that, the more totally contingent creatures are, the greater God appears. Yet it is of a piece with this that these philosophers taught that creatures cannot reveal to us an omnipotent Creator; it was the philosophers who granted some necessity to creatures in existing and operating who taught that philosophy can disclose to us the existence of an omnipotent God.

Let us now see examples of what the divine power philosophers thought that God could do against His wisdom and goodness. Since we are grouping together a great many writers, however, it will be understood that we are dealing with typical doctrines, not ones each of which was held by everyone.

1. In the physical order they held that God could change a material being into a spirit, and one spirit into another; that He could change an immortal soul into a mortal one; that He could change an accident into a substance; that He could cause the same body, and even a human person, to exist in many places at the same time; and that when this happens a person could be killed in one location and not in another, be in the state of grace in one location and not in another, be in heaven in one location and in hell in another, and even constitute a whole army.

2. In the order of knowledge they held that we could sense objects which are not present just as if they were; that we could be unsure that what appears to be a cause really is one; and that God could make an intellect which does not accept the principle of non-contradiction. (They did not point out, however, that, if this were so, we cannot now be sure that the intellect we have is right in acceding to its nature and accepting the principle of non-contradiction, and that, if the principle of non-contradiction goes, we can be sure of nothing.)

3. As concerns the intellect and will, they taught that
there could be acts of intellection and volition with no subjects
performing these acts, that acts of intellection and volition could
exist without objects, and that the will could desire something
unknown to the intellect.

4. As concerns the moral order, they taught that God could
have given us no moral code whatever, that the one He has
given us could be completely different from what it is, that
God could have required us to hate Him, and that the only
real moral value is obedience. They taught that morality is
determined ultimately not by the divine intellect but by the
divine will.

5. As regards God's knowledge of the future, some said
that future contingents are so contingent that, until they happen,
they could be otherwise. As a result, if God has revealed
some of them, for example the Last Judgment, or the Resurrection
of Bodies, He can have spoken falsely, and therefore God
can deceive us. Others said that creatures are so under divine
power that freedom is impossible, and that all human beings
are predestined from eternity to heaven or hell irrespective
of a consideration of their foreseen merits or demerits.

6. In the supernatural order they taught that God could
have assumed a non-rational nature, such as that of a stone
or an ass. And that God could sin and be damned in a
rational nature He assumed.

7. As concerns sanctifying grace and love of God, they
held   that, under God's present arrangement, these are required
in order to be pleasing to God, to be able to merit, and
to attain eternal life. But they claimed that, by His absolute
power, God could dispense with this. He could require nothing
in a person, or something other than grace or love, such as
faith, or a physical quality such as curly hair. Since no
created thing can make demands on God, He is not required
to accept a person who loves Him or reject a person who

hates Him. They said that God could reject and damn someone who loves Him, even one of the Blessed in heaven, and reward with eternal life someone who hates Him, even someone in hell. Thus mortal sin could be the cause of justification, and charity the cause of damnation. As justification is simply acceptance by God, so rejection is simply non-acceptance by Him. Nothing in the soul need correspond to either of these. Being in the state of mortal sin is merely being subject to eternal separation from God and eternal punishment; it implies no deformity in the soul. Thus God could forgive mortal sin without a person being repentant.

8. As regards the Beatific Vision, they taught that the Blessed cannot be sure that it will last, even if God has revealed to them that it will. They taught that one could see in this Vision the divine essence without the Persons, one Person without another, the divine essence without its attributes, or one attribute without another. And that one could have the face-to-face vision of God without taking any joy in it, indeed, while hating God and suffering the torments of the damned.

9. In addition they taught that God could annihilate any creature at any moment, even a rational creature, and even that God could undo the past and make it so that it never existed.

*****

One effect of these doctrines was to trivialize the natural and supernatural orders actually established by God. For example, to say that the present moral law is arbitrary, that love of God can be evil and hatred of God good, that God can annihilate any creature, and that God can undo the past is to take away from the importance of the moral law and of the whole of creation.

Another effect was to make men less sure of the significance of life. If an immortal soul can be rendered mortal, if God

can tell us falsehoods, if we can be predestined to heaven
or hell irrespective of our free actions, if even the Blessed
can be sent to hell, and if we can be annihilated at any
moment, what confidence can we have that life is worthwhile?

*****

We now know much more than we did ten years ago
concerning the history of this doctrine of divine absolute power.
Though there were instances of it in the twelfth century, it
seems to have started in the thirteenth century only after the
death of St. Thomas Aquinas (1274). Aquinas showed that
he was familiar with the notion of divine absolute power.
He thought, however, that it was not a useful notion because
God cannot do anything contrary to His goodness or wisdom.[1]
God could, for example, according to His absolute power, reveal
to us something that could be false,[2] or assume a non-rational
or an angelic nature,[3] or annihilate a creature,[4] or change the
will of an angel,[5] or reveal to someone that he will be damned;[6]
but in actual fact God could never really do these things
because they would be contrary to His wisdom or goodness.

The appeal to divine absolute power as a real possibility
began after Aquinas with Duns Scotus (1266-1308). A recent
article[7] has shown this, and also that other Franciscans followed
Scotus, and went further along this road. These Franciscans
can be placed in three groups. One group continues this
trend of Scotus, but its members do not belong to a particular
school, for example, Peter Aureole (his *Sentences* date from
1316 to 1318). Another group are early Scotists, such as
John de Bassolis (his *Sentences* were composed in 1313), Francis
of Meyronnes (his *Sentences* were written 1320-21), and William
Rubio (his *Sentences* were completed well before 1334). These
men were uninfluenced by William of Ockham. The third
group are William of Ockham (his *Sentences* date from 1317
to 1319) and his followers, for example, Adam Wodeham, his
chief disciple (his *Sentences* were written 1330-1333). Ockhamists
were prone to speculate on divine absolute power, but they

were not the only Franciscans like this; there were Scotists and other non-Ockhamists also, independently of them and even prior to them.

Another article[8] has shown that not only Franciscans followed Scotus's lead. Durandus de Sancto Poricano (his *Sentences* were composed 1307-08) and Robert Holcot (his *Sentences* were revised in 1336) were two Dominicans who did so. Durandus wrote before Ockham; Holcot wrote after him and was very much influenced by him, perhaps because he had been already influenced by his Dominican confrere.

We thus see that frequent recourse to divine absolute power was widespread by the end of the first quarter of the fourteenth century. Many texts from this period are still not transcribed, but when transcribed will no doubt reveal just as great an interest in concentrating on divine absolute power. An interesting text is the *Sentences* of the Benedictine Robert Graystanes, composed c. 1325. Greystanes used the notion of divine absolute power to do away with a great deal of necessity in the created universe, and as a result taught a deep scepticism.[9]

In the next fifty years, concern with divine absolute power was omnipresent. We find it in the Franciscan John Went (his *Sentences* were written in 1338-39)[10] and in the Augustinians Thomas of Strasbourg and Alphonsus Vargas of Toledo (their *Sentences* date from 1335-37 and 1344-45 respectively).[11] Propositions of Nicholas of Autrecourt, a secular priest, and the Cistercian John of Mirecourt, some of which dealt with divine absolute power, were condemned at Paris in 1346 and 1347 respectively. Richard Fitzralph, a secular priest (his *Sentences* were composed in 1328), the Benedictine Monachus Niger (his *Sentences* date from 1337 to 1341), the Carmelite John Titleshale (his *Sentences* were composed between 1340 and 1350), and the secular priest Nicholas Aston (his *Sentences* were composed c. 1350) used the doctrine of divine absolute power to rule out necessity in the created universe and thus teach scepticism.[12] The Carmelite Osbert of Pickenham (fl. 1360) used this notion to show that

God, if hypostatically united to a rational nature, could sin.[13] And his Carmelite confrere in Paris, Michael Aiguani, whose *Sentences* were composed 1362-63, held many of the doctrines listed earlier.[14]

We find in the *Sentences* (1365-70) of the Franciscan Andrew of Novo Castro the most thorough attempt, by an appeal to divine absolute power, to remove necessity from the moral order and to make morality purely arbitrary on God's part.[15]

And we find the *ne plus ultra* of obsession with divine absolute power in the *Sentences* of Peter of Ailly, written in 1376-77. Peter (1350-1420), the most famous churchman of his day, used the threat of divine absolute power to teach total philosophical scepticism. The only certain truths, he said, are the principle of non-contradiction and the principle that, if God commands us to do something, we must obey Him. And Peter implicitly denied the certainty of the first of these principles, which denial of course destroys the certainty of the second. No greater proof of the destructive power of recourse to divine absolute power can be found than Peter's *Sentences*.[16]

But recourse to this power was to continue strong until the early sixteenth century. If we study the *Sentences* of Scotists and Ockhamists on the eve of the Protestant Reformation, we find these thinkers quite preoccupied with divine absolute power. This is true, for example, of the Scotists (all Franciscan) Nicholas de Orbellis (d. 1475), Paul Scriptoris (d. 1505), and Nicholas Denyse (d. 1509), as well as of the Ockhamists Gabriel Biel (a member of the Brethren of the Common Life, d. 1495) and of the secular priests John Major (d. 1550) and James Almain (d. 1515).[17]

These doctrines of divine absolute power had an effect on Martin Luther (d. 1546). As is evident with modern technology, when something is able to be done, someone sooner or later does it, no matter how serious the consequences. And, in the late Middle Ages, with these powerful theoretical possibilities around, someone was bound to say that what could have been actually is. This is what we find in the case of Luther, concerning the topic of justification.

The scholastic theologians most cherished by Luther were William of Ockham, Peter of Ailly, and Gabriel Biel. Melanchthon wrote that Luther knew the latter two almost by heart and that he read Ockham frequently and for long periods. The theology Luther encountered thus contained the doctrine of divine absolute power we have been describing. If he had wanted to teach that what is pleasing to God *par excellence is* not charity but faith, he would have had to go a step beyond his mentors, but one can hardly imagine a theology more likely to have invited this step.

Now, why did Luther take the step? He himself has told us. He was very worried about his salvation. He agonized over it. He wanted to be absolutely sure that he was saved. There were two things bothering him. One was the Catholic teaching, to be reinforced by the Council of Trent, that we cannot be absolutely sure that we are in the state of grace, absolutely sure that we love God above all things. Moreover, we have the effects of original sin, are prone to sin, and cannot be sure that we will not commit serious sin. Luther was almost in despair over this matter. But he tells us that the problem was resolved for him by an experience in the tower of his friary in Wittenberg, during the academic year 1518-19. What he saw is that justification is produced not by charity but by faith. He wrote that he was filled with joy and that he began to interpret all the New Testament according to this new insight.

Why was Luther filled with joy? Because his insight solved both parts of his problem. First, it is easier to be sure that we have faith than it is to be sure that we have charity. Secondly, according to traditional Catholic teaching, faith is compatible with mortal sin. Luther was to teach that,

when God justifies us, He doesn't take away our sins; we
remain in them.   And, even if we commit mortal sins, we
are justified as long as we have faith.   "If we commit fornication
or murder a thousand times a day," Luther wrote to Melanchthon
on August 1, 1521, "we remain justified as long as we have
faith."   Luther therefore could be confident that he was in
God's grace, and he didn't have to fear losing it by sin.

What Luther did was to claim as a fact what the theologians
he read claimed as a possibility, namely, that God could justify
us not by charity but by anything He wished, such as faith.
What Luther had to do next was to show that this was actually
the teaching of Scripture, as he had seen in the tower.   Luther
thought that he was able to achieve this.   The final thing
he had to do was to show that this was traditional Catholic
teaching.   He realized that this was impossible and therefore
he had to claim that popes and general councils could be
wrong.   So he set about to interpret the New Testament in
such a way as to reduce or nullify the authority of the pope
and even of councils.[18]

The Council of Trent was called to respond to Lutheranism.
Its tools would not have been adequate if only Scotism and
Ockhamism were at hand to answer Luther's theology of justification.
But fortunately there was Thomism.   If we look at the best-
known Thomists of the pre-Reformation period, John Capreolus
(d. 1444) and Cardinal Cajetan (d. 1534), we see that they
strenuously opposed the divine power philosophers in many
matters, and particularly in the matter of justification.

Capreolus called heretical the doctrine that God in an assumed
nature could sin or could be damned.   He said also that
God could not assume the nature of a damned person.   And
he taught that God necessarily approves of grace and charity,
and necessarily rewards good works.   This necessity, he said,
does not arise from what God owes to creatures but from
what He owes, as it were, to His own goodness and justice.[19]

And Cardinal Cajetan vigorously opposed the applications of the notion of divine absolute power in the matter of the Incarnation, grace and charity, and divine foreknowledge.[20]

Thus these two leading Thomists were faithful to their master concerning the notion of divine absolute power. Only Thomists withstood the almost universally popular doctrine.

The legend that Aquinas's *Summa Theologiae* was placed on the altar, along with the Bible, at the church in Trent in which the Council was held, was a well-entrenched legend, lasting for hundreds of years, misleading even Pius XI (in 1923), but it is not true. That is to say, it is not literally true; what it implies *is* true. Aquinas's authority at the Council was great, and many interventions brought in his theology, particularly the interventions of the 135 Dominicans who took part in the Council, 31 of them bishops. (Remember, the Council lasted eighteen years.) During the last year of the Council (1563), on the feast of St. Thomas Aquinas, the preacher, the Dominican John Gallon, said that, though Aquinas had died on his way to a General Council in 1274, he had been present at the Church's councils ever since.

Four years after the Council ended, the Dominican pope Pius V praised Aquinas for his influence at the Council and made him a Doctor of the Church. He wrote: "In the providence of Almighty God many heresies which arose were checked and were scattered in confusion through the power and truth of the teaching of the Angelic Doctor. This often happened previously and happened again, as is clear, in the sacred decrees of the Council of Trent. Therefore we declare that the memory of this man should be held sacred, this man by whose merits the world is freed daily from dangerous errors."[21]

It seems to me incredible that most of the Scholastics for two hundred years could have adopted the doctrine of divine absolute power they accepted. I am amazed at the time, talent, and energy expended on what they thought might have been, with a corresponding downplaying of what is. This paralleled in the theoretical order what was going on in the Church in the practical order: a neglect of the actual state of things. It is to the credit of Luther that he opposed some of the scholastic philosophy he knew. But it is to his debit that what he did take from it were some of its worst teachings.

We should be grateful that the Council of Trent had a better knowledge of scholasticism than Luther had, and that Thomism was present to correct some of the teachings Luther had followed.

St. Peter's Seminary
University of Western Ontario
London, Ontario

NOTES

1. *Summa Theologiae*, I, 25, 5, ad 1; *Sentences*, III, d. 1, q. 2, a. 3.

2. *Sentences*, III, d. 24, a. 1.

3. Ibid., d. 2, q. 1.

4. *Quodlibeta*, IV, q. 3, a. 1.

5. *De Malo*, q. 16, a. 5, ratio 13.

6. *De Veritate*, q. 23, a. 8, ad 2.

7. L. A. Kennedy, "Early Fourteenth-Century Franciscans and Divine Absolute Power," *Franciscan Studies*, 49 (1989).

8. L. A. Kennedy, "Two Early-Fourteenth-Century Dominicans and Divine Absolute Power," forthcoming.

9. A question of his *Sentences* (the first question of the First Commentary) has been transcribed from its copy in the notebook of the Carmelite Stephen Patrington. See L. A. Kennedy, "Late Fourteenth-Century Philosophical Scepticism at Oxford," *Vivarium*, 23 (1985), 124-151. For a description of Greystanes' *Sentences* see L. A. Kennedy, "Robert Graystanes' *Commentary on the Sentences*," *Recherches de Théologie ancienne et médiévale*, 53 (1986), 185-189.

10. L. A. Kennedy and M. E. Romano, "John Went, O.F.M., and Divine Omnipotence," *Franciscan Studies*, 47 (1987), 138-170.

11. L. A. Kennedy, "Two Augustinians and Nominalism," *Augustiniana*, 38 (1988), 118-128.

12. L. A. Kennedy, "Philosophical Scepticism in England in the Mid-Fourteenth-Century," *Vivarium*, 21 (1983), 35-57.

13. L. A. Kennedy, "Osbert of Pickenham, O.Carm. (fl. 1360), on the Absolute Power of God," *Carmelus*, 35 (1988), 178-225.

14. L. A. Kennedy, "Michael Aiguani, O.Carm., and Divine Absolute Power," *Carmelus*, 36 (1989).

15. L. A. Kennedy, "Andrew of Novo Castro, O.F.M., and the Moral Law," *Franciscan Studies*, 48 (1988).

16. L. A. Kennedy, *Peter of Ailly and the Harvest of Fourteenth-Century Philosophy*, (Lewiston, N. Y., 1986).

17. L. A. Kennedy, "The Fifteenth Century and Divine Absolute Power," *Vivarium*, 27 (1989).

18. L. A. Kennedy, "Martin Luther and Scholastic Theology," forthcoming.

19. Ibid.

20. Ibid.

21. A. Walz, *I Domenicani al Concilio di Trento* (Rome, 1961), 314-315, 360-361, 425-428.

THE PROBLEM OF CERTITUDE: REFLECTIONS ON THE *GRAMMAR OF ASSENT**

Thomas D. Sullivan

It is sometimes said by modern critics that John Henry Newman's *Grammar of Assent* does not argue a case, but merely depicts what it means to hold a belief, religious or non-religious. This idea of the *Grammar* arises in part from Newman's modest claims for a work filled with astute psychological observation. But contemporaries of Newman, such as W. G. Ward, well understood his fundamental purpose. "Newman," Ward wrote, "deserves the warm gratitude of his co-religionists, were it only as being the first to fix Catholic attention on what is certainly the one chief stronghold of philosophical objectors against the Church. . ." And, Ward continued, Newman "deserves still more gratitude for the singular power of argument and felicity of illustration he has brought to his task." (Ward, 244)

By the "chief stronghold" Ward meant the charge that Catholicism requires intellectual dishonesty. We are obliged to be intellectually responsible, proportioning belief to evidence. But whatever evidence exists for the claim that God has revealed his mind to us, the evidence cannot possibly be strong enough to warrant absolute confidence in those who claim to be messengers from God. Nonetheless, the Church requires faith, firm belief in the absence of irresistible proof, that God has spoken to us through these messengers. This in itself shows Catholicism is false.

A similar objection, of course, could be brought against any religion that requires firm intellectual commitment to received doctrine. From John Locke, whose remarks on revelation in Book IV of the *Essay Concerning Human Understanding* occasioned much of what we find in the *Grammar*, to W. K. Clifford, Bertrand Russell, and Brand Blanshard, the demand to equate belief to the evidence has always represented a challenge to faith *as such*. In defending the belief of Catholics against the "chief stronghold of objectors," Newman was thus defending all who are disposed to accept with reverence the word of God through appointed messengers.[1]

But what, precisely, was Newman's defense?

It is not easy to say. The *Grammar* suggests several distinct answers. My purpose in the following is to try to disengage from better known, but faulty arguments the only argument that seems to me correct.

I.

The first task, then, is to set out the objection more formally than Newman does himself. Since the argument proceeds on *a priori* grounds, without troubling to examine the evidence for religious belief, let us refer to it as the *A Priori* Objection. Following Newman, we will express the objection in terms of Catholicism, though, as just noted, a similar argument could be brought to bear on a number of faiths.

The A Priori Objection

*1. It is immoral not to proportion belief in a proposition to the evidence for the proposition. [Call this the Proportionality Precept].

*2. Catholicism requires absolute adherence to some propositions for which there does not exist compelling evidence.

*3. If adherence to a proposition is absolute while the evidence for it uncompelling, the belief is disproportionate to the evidence.

4. Catholicism requires belief disproportionate to the evidence. [From 2,3]

5. Catholicism requires its members to do something immoral. [1,4]

*6. No religion that requires its members to do something immoral is true.

7. Catholicism is not true. [From 5,6]

The starred propositions are the basic assumptions from which the rest flows. Let us consider these assumptions.

II.

It will prove convenient to work backwards, starting with *6. Newman does not deny *6. If the morality of a religion is low, that by itself shows it is false. ". . . [N]o religion is from God which contradicts our sense of right and wrong. (*Grammar*, hereafter *G*, 318) He continues, "The precepts of a religion certainly may be absolutely immoral; a religion which simply commanded us to lie, or to have a community of wives, would *ipso facto* forfeit all claim to a divine origin." (*G*, 319) We are drawn to Christianity in part by the very beauty of its moral doctrine; it must come from heaven.

So much, then, for *6.

III.

That brings us to proposition *3—If adherence to a proposition
is absolute while the evidence for it is uncompelling, the belief
is disproportionate to the evidence.

Newman variously speaks of devout belief as "unqualified,"
"absolute," and "unconditional." The main attribute of such
belief, whatever it is called, is that it is *undoubting*. We
may be convinced beyond doubt that something is so, convinced
beyond doubt that it is not so, or somewhere in between.
Affirmative conviction lies at one extreme.

Similarly, evidence ranges from being overwhelmingly in
favor of a proposition to being overwhelmingly against it. When
evidence is overwhelmingly in favor of a proposition, it might
be called "compelling"—we are *compelled* to believe. Commonly
cited sources of compelling evidence include internal and external
perception, axioms of thought, and the products of short demonstrations
from the same. To these we must add with Newman the
sort of evidence that leads us to infer with complete confidence
that *England is an island* and *There are other minds.*

Absolute, undoubting adherence to a proposition can be
produced by compelling evidence. The summit of belief is
equal to the summit of evidence. But absolute assent can
exist in the absence of compelling evidence. The summit
of belief exceeds the evidence. So, there is a disproportion.
Proposition *3 is truism.

IV.

Proposition *2 is the claim that Catholicism requires absolute
adherence, i.e., undoubting belief, in some propositions for which
there does not exist compelling evidence. There are three
points here: (A) That Catholicism requires belief in propositions,
(B) the quality of the belief is that of absolute adherence,
(C) that the evidence is not compelling.

(A) *Propositions as Objects of Belief*

(A) is obvious on the face of it. Catholicism has definite creeds and defined propositions.

Of course there are religiously minded persons who think that genuine religion has nothing to do with fixed propositions and unqualified assent. Faith is not a matter of accepting propositions, but an affair of the heart, a relationship to a Person. Granted, when talking about faith we are talking about something more than mere acceptance of propositions. Propositions are only vehicles for thinking about God in certain ways. But it is hard to imagine how one could fully commit oneself to God without believing *that* there is such a being as God, any more than one could resolve to go to Boston without believing that there is a Boston.

In any event, Newman did not try to escape from the *A Priori* Objection by claiming that Catholicism does not offer distinct propositions as objects of belief. Quite the opposite. Newman claimed the marvelous growth of doctrine was a sign of the divine origin of the Church. (*G*, 327-28)

(B) *The Requirement of Unreserved Assent*

Some Christians see faith as a risk. Doubt is a necessary element of true faith. Newman allows that a measure of devotion is possible without conviction. But "[s]acrifice of wealth, name, or position, faith and hope, self-conquest, communion with the spiritual world, presuppose a real hold and habitual intuition of the objects of Revelation, which is certitude under another name." (*G*, 180) We recite creeds that begin not with "I believe the existence of God has some probability," but "I believe in God." Our prayer is not, "Oh God, if there is a God, save my soul, if I have a soul," but, "Help me, Yaweh my God, save me since you love me."

Of course this does not mean that faith is without difficulties. Faith, after all, is faith—not knowledge. But as Newman observed, ten thousand difficulties do not make one doubt, any more than a hundred ponies make a horse. Nor does it mean that the faithful cannot investigate these difficulties, as we are now, or acknowledge their force. It is rather that we are to remain confident in the word of God, to pray for light, and remain within it, responding to the movements of grace.

Whatever one thinks of the wisdom of this requirement of Catholicism, Catholicism does indeed require of those with the gift of faith unconditional assent to its creeds.[2]

(C) *Compelling Evidence*

That brings us to the third point (C): the evidence for the propositions is disproportionate to the belief.

Here faithful Catholics sometimes balk. Raised in an anti-fideist tradition that lays great stress on evidence and natural theology, Catholics often tend to transmute faith into knowledge. From Aquinas' five ways, based on such features of the world as its contingency and order, we arrive at God's existence and divine attributes, including his unfailing truthfulness. Then, since God has revealed the mysteries of Christianity to us, and the truth of that revelation is secured by God's veracity, the revelation is certainly true. Q.E.D.

A moment of serious reflection, however, should dispel that illusion. First, we certainly don't want to say that only philosophers and theologians can properly have faith. As Aquinas himself observes, only the tiniest minority of believers with the desire, talent, and opportunity to solve all the knotty philosophical problems can come to know the existence and attributes of

God through natural theology. Faith seldom originates from philosophical reflection.

But even when it does, philosophy can only carry us so far. It cannot make revealed truths evident. Suppose you demonstrate that God exists and cannot deceive. It follows that if God has revealed that he is triune, then God is triune—*if* God has revealed this. But while evidence exists for the credibility of the revelation, it is not compelling evidence— evidence that *compels* assent. The claims of apostle, gospel, or church to speak as the oracle of God are not backed by irresistible evidence.

What, though, of the "Illative Sense?" Does not Newman show how we may attain certitude in these matters through a mode of knowing more personal, more concrete than what could be captured by paper logic? Why not say with Newman that the mind, operating on antecedent and converging probabilities, can reach certitude about the divinity of Christ in the same way it can about the existence of India? (*G*, 262) Though we cannot set out our arguments in the style of Euclid, that's also true of propositions such as "England is an island" and "I was born of a woman." A mountain of implicit evidence backs these propositions with a cogency on a par or nearly on a par with a proof in Euclid. As Charles Frederick Harrold expresses it in the introduction of his edition of the *Grammar*,

> [I]t was Newman's doctrine of the "illative
> sense," which seemed to many readers an
> admirable solution to the old problem of
> reason, faith and certitude.

The "illative sense" may be defined as the spontaneous divination by the mind in concrete matters that a conclusion is inevitable, if it is felt to be "as good as proved," even though not determined by a process of reasoning logically complete. (*G*, xvii)

Harrold could point to much in Newman to support this
view. (See especially *G*, 262)   And there are times when
the reader of the *Grammar*, swept along by the great beauty
and power of Newman's argument for Christianity, may well
feel that revelation is as good as proved.   But for all that
Newman offers us in the *Grammar*, it cannot be fairly said
it is shown there that implicit and personal evidence confers
on a belief such as "The Church is infallible," certitude comparable
to that enjoyed by propositions such as "I am a mortal being"
or "There is an India." With respect to many everyday judgments,
the evidence is so compelling that we feel, as Wittgenstein
puts it, "If I don't trust *this* evidence why should I trust
any evidence." (*On Certainty*, n. 672, 89) Everything speaks
for the fact, nothing against it.   But this is not the way
it is with religious belief.   There are genuine difficulties.   I
am not saying that one cannot be legitimately as certain of
the one as of the other.   I am saying rather that the certitude
in the case of religious belief does not entirely rest on evidence.

Faith is not knowledge.   Evidence there is, but what steels
religious belief is not evidence alone.[3]

Despite, then, what some commentators say, Newman cannot
solve the problem of certitude in religious matters merely by
appealing to the illative sense as a personal mode of proof
in practical matters.   The evidence is disproportionate to the
assent.   Newman's contributions to the psychology of assent
are very considerable, but they cannot serve the function of
showing how to transmute faith into knowledge.

V.

And so we are driven back to *1, the Proportionality Precept:
It is immoral not to proportion belief to the evidence for
the belief.

A. *Various Attacks on the Proportionality Precept*

Philosophers and theologians have attacked the Proportionality Precept in a number of ways.

It is sometimes argued that this precept, promoted by the scientifically minded of the Enlightenment, undercuts science itself. The history of science is replete with success stories of theorists sticking with their beliefs against a mountain of evidence to the contrary. Other responses include the dismissal of the need for any evidence to justify the rationality of religious belief and the claim that believing isn't under our control, so it is not under the jurisdiction of a moral rule.

None of these, it seems to me, is adequate. Unfortunately, a number of Newman's suggestions are not any better.

Newman complains that the Proportionality Precept is meaningless. Locke tells us there is to be no "surplusage of *assurance beyond* the degree of that evidence." But assent, Newman insists, does not admit of degrees. (*G*, 123 ff.) "We might as well talk of degrees of truth as of degrees of assent." (*G*, 131) Assent by definition is unconditional acceptance of a truth. (*G*, 130) Assent is an all or nothing affair. One can no more partially assent to a proposition than partially touch something.

But as H. H. Price shows in his Gifford Lectures, by this maneuver Newman at best gains a small verbal victory over Locke. (*Belief*, 130-157) The substantive problem remains untouched, even if we give up Locke's wording of his point in terms of "degrees of assent." One might very well say, "Fine, let us stipulate that 'assent' means complete adhesion to a proposition; so one cannot assent by degrees. But certainly there are well recognized psychological states between being dead certain that something is the case and dead certain that it is not. Most of the time we are somewhere in between, *leaning* toward one view and away from another. The Proportionality

Precept, then, may be rephrased, using expressions such as
"lean towards," or "incline towards," or "confident to the extent
that." Locke is not talking nonsense.

So the Proportionality Precept is meaningful. Can it be
followed? W. G. Ward thought that Newman's solution consisted
in showing that it cannot. As Newman showed in fine detail,
too much of the evidence for what we believe is implicit,
and so we cannot get all the evidence before the mind in
order to assent to the proper degree. (Ward, 250) Again,
the solution won't do. True, most of my evidence for, say,
my friend's honesty is implicit. If I tried to make a list
of times when he has proved himself honest, it would be
embarrassingly short. But I know that there have been thousands
of times when he has proved honest. I know I have, though
I cannot give, mountains of evidence for the proposition. On
the other hand, I can't say the same about the first person
I meet on the street. Similarly, I am sure for more reasons
than I can possibly articulate that India exists, while I know
that I have little or no implicit evidence for the existence
of the latest hypothetical entity concocted by physicists trying
to explain the superconductivity of certain ceramics. So I
can, and I do—at least roughly—proportion my belief to the
evidence I know I have. An objector to the Proportionality
Precept might as well say, "The rule to proportion your spending
to your wealth is impossible to follow, because nobody knows
precisely how much he or she is worth. Much of one's
holdings can't be precisely fixed. And who knows at a given
moment exactly how much change is rattling around in the
pocket?"

B. *Newman on the Duty to Believe*

So none of these solutions seem to work. But Newman
has a better argument against the Proportionality Precept. His
point of departure is an extension of Aristotle's doctrine of
phronesis to cover believing. (*G*, 268)

The idea, I take it, is this. To believe is to act; therefore the choice to believe is properly subject to guidance by an acquired habit, formed and matured by practice and experience. (*G*, 268) The wise—Newman quotes the *Nicomachean Ethics*—"expect exactness in every class of subject, according as the nature of the thing admits." (*G*, 314) In religious matters, we cannot intelligently expect argument on a par with what is found in mathematics.

> As in mathematics we are justified by the dictate of nature in withholding our assent from an undemonstrated conclusion, so by a like dictate we are not justified, in practical matters, especially of religious inquiry, in waiting till such logical demonstration is ours, but are bound in conscience to seek truth and to look for certainty by modes of proof, which when reduced to the shape of formal propositions, fail to satisfy the severe requisitions of science. (*G*, 313)

So the personal act of believing may well express the excellent practical judgment of a mind that sees enough of the evidence to realize it would be wrong to refuse to honor a divine truth.

The trouble with the Proportionality Precept, then, is just that it exempts one activity—believing—from the governance of prudence. No abstract rule can determine just under what circumstances something is to be believed or believed without reservation.

> The authoritative oracle, which is to decide our path, is something more searching and manifold than such jejune generalizations as treatises can give, which are most distinct and clear when we least need them. It is seated in the mind of the individual, who

is thus his own law, his own teacher, and
his own judge in those special cases of
duty which are personal to him. (*G*, 269)

This is not to say there is nothing to the Proportionality
Precept. Practical wisdom should not disdain evidence. But
the Precept is simplistically stated, and it is not at all clear
that it can be amended in such a way as to prove unexceptional
in all circumstances. Practical wisdom often must judge concrete
matters in the absence of proximate universal norms. If believing
is acting, it must be regulated in the same way, by practical
wisdom taking into account circumstances.

Newman's complaint against the Proportionality Precept seems
entirely justified. Imagine you are a juror in a civil trial
between Smith and Jones. Before you hear any evidence,
Smith and Jones have an equal chance of being right. Now
Smith tells the tale—his way of course. And so as Smith
concludes his testimony, the evidence favors Smith. What
should you do? Immediately side with Smith before Jones
gets to tell her side of the story? Of course not. In these
matters we do not *immediately* proportion our belief to the
weight of the evidence.

This exception to the Proportionality Precept rule is neither
small nor insignificant. It draws attention to the fact that
punctilious adherence to the Proportionality Precept would operate
contrary to the ends of human existence, including the very
adjudication of the truth.

The example of the case of law may suggest that wisdom
always dictates deferring a decision until all the evidence is
in. But no such rule is practical or wise. Waiting until
"all the evidence is in" means postponing marriage, benevolent
acts, choosing a career—just about anything of worth—until
it is too late. And are we to wait until all the evidence
is in before deciding whether the rule to wait is measured
by "all the evidence?"

The proper response to evidence is a matter of practical wisdom. Timing is but one circumstance of the act. The object is another. What does the belief bear on? The fidelity of one's mate? Othello's belief in the faithfulness of Desdamona? The integrity of one's parents or friends?

With respect to religious belief, what we should ask ourselves is not whether the evidence establishes beyond possible doubt whether God has revealed a truth to us, but rather whether the evidence is sufficient for us to judge *that we have an obligation to believe what is taught us.* In a letter written to Mrs. Katherine Ward fourteen years after the first appearance of the *Grammar of Assent*, Newman puts it this way.

> Reason does not prove that Catholicism is true, as it proves that mathematical conclusions are true . . . but it proves that there is a *case* for it so strong that we see we ought to accept it. There may be many difficulties which we cannot answer, but still we see on the whole that grounds are sufficient for conviction. This is not the same thing as conviction. If conviction were unavoidable, we might be said to be forced to believe as we are forced to mathematical conclusions; but while there is enough evidence for conviction, whether we *will* be convinced or not rests with ourselves . . . .
>
> *You can believe what you will*; the only question is whether your reason tells you that you *ought* to believe . . . (12 October 1884. *Letters*, 289)

In sum, Newman rejects the Proportionality Precept, and with it the *A Priori* Objection, because believing is acting, and acting becomes obligatory on less than certain evidence. The way is thus open to another way of considering the claims of a revealed religion.

With his abhorrence of "paper logic," Newman would never dream of expressing the argument in this way. But it seems to me that this is what the argument comes to.

N1 If it seems (highly) probable both that an end is obligatory and an action is indispensable to the end, then the action is itself obligatory. [If it seems probable to a firefighter that it is obligatory to rescue a person from a burning building and this can only be done by raising a ladder, then it is obligatory for the firefighter to raise a ladder.]

N2 If God has revealed something as true, then it is true.

N3 It may seem (highly) probable to someone (properly disposed to hear the evidence) that God has revealed that a certain end is an obligatory end (union with himself) and an action indispensable (absolute adherence to his teachings.)

N4 It may seem probable to someone that union with God is an obligatory end and absolute adherence to teaching indispensable. [From 2,3]

N5 Absolute adherence is obligatory (for anyone who sees the relevant evidence.) [From 1,4]

Expressing Newman's argument this way permits us to see how the Illative Sense may contribute to faith, without claiming for it a power to transmute faith into knowledge. The proper role of the Illative sense is to furnish the judgment that in all likelihood God has revealed the received message— N3.

The reasoning is practical, as it should be. But it is not pragmatic. This is not an argument in the mode of Pascal's Wager.[4] Reflection on the evidence must *favor* religious belief. Truth, after all, is the very purpose for which the world was made, and it must not be sacrificed to any pragmatic end. But we should not wait until we *see* the whole truth of Christ's doctrine. For we cannot arrive at the whole truth without first attaching ourselves to the Light. As Newman said, more than thirty years before writing his *Grammar*, "Wisdom is the last gift of the Spirit, and Faith the first." (*Sermons Preached Before the University of Oxford*, 294).

College of St. Thomas
Saint Paul, Minnesota

NOTES

*I wish to thank Greg Coulter, Mary Hayden, and Thomas Russman for helpful comments on a version of this paper presented as the Aquinas Lecture at the University of St. Thomas, Houston, in January of 1989.

This article extends the treatment of Newman's views adopted in "Adequate Evidence for Religious Belief," in *Thomistic Papers IV*.

1.　It should go without saying that this remark does not suggest religious indifferentism.　Newman firmly believed, as do I, that the *"organum investigandi* given us for gaining religious truth...lead[s]...to Catholicity." [*G*, 389].

2.　First Vatican Council, Session 3, April 24, 1870, *Dogmatic Constitution on the Catholic Faith*, ch. 3.　Cited by Lawler, Wuerl, and Lawler, *The Teachings of Christ*, 296 for claim that "[T]hose who have received the faith under the teaching authority of the Church can never have a just reason to change the same faith or to call it into doubt."

3.　It is the will moved by grace. Some Catholics reject this, arguing that the role of grace is to confer illumination sufficient to render the fact of revelation evident.　The role of the will, on this account, is only to dispose the person for illumination.　Aquinas, it is noted, calls faith *knowledge.* He does, but he also says, "Faith is said to be less than scientific knowledge because faith, unlike science, lacks vision of the fact, though it has the same firmness."　(Fides) "dicitur tamen esse infra scientiam quia non habet visionem sicut scientia quamvis habeat ita firmam adhaesionem...." (*Disputed Questions on Truth*, q. 14, a. 2)　The point deserves more attention than we can give it here.　Those who think that illumination does render the fact of revelation evident may pursue what follows as an alternative account of the justification of religious belief.

4. Pascal's Wager Argument is an instance of the now standard process of probabilistic decision calculated on the basis of expected-value. The Wager is intended to work even if the probability of Christianity's being true may be low. See, Rescher, especially 15-16.

REFERENCES

Newman

Newman, John Henry. *An Essay in Aid of A Grammar of Assent*, ed. by Charles Frederick Harrold, (New York, London, Toronto: Longmans, Green and Co., 1947).

Newman, John Henry. *Letters and Diaries of John Henry Newman*, Volume XII, ed. Charles Stephen Dessain, (London: Thomas Nelson and Sons Ltd., 1962).

Newman, John Henry. *Fifteen Sermons Preached Before The University of Oxford*, (London, New York, and Bombay: Longmans, Green, and Co., 1898).

Other Sources

Lawler, Wuerl, and Lawler, eds., *The Teaching of Christ*, (Huntington, 1976).

Price, H. H., *Belief*, (London: Humanities Press, 1969).

Rescher, Nicholas. *Pascal's Wager*, (Notre Dame: University of Notre Dame Press, 1985).

Ward, William G. *Essays on the Philosophy of Theism*, Vol. II, ed. by Wilfrid Ward, (London: Kegan Paul, Trench & Co., 1884).

Wittgenstein, Ludwig. *On Certainty*, trans. by G. E. M. Anscombe and G. H. von Wright, (New York: Harper Torchbooks, 1969).

A FAITH OF TRUE PROPORTIONS: REPLY TO SULLIVAN

Thomas A. Russman, OFM Cap

Thomas Sullivan has introduced us to a fascinating discussion by setting out to answer what he calls "the *a priori* objection to religious faith." I will be discussing two of the premises of this *a priori* objection, the same ones that Sullivan himself picked out for extensive treatment.

Premise 1: It is immoral not to proportion belief in a proposition to the evidence for the proposition. Sullivan calls this the proportionality precept. A small quibble—I am uncomfortable with Sullivan's use of the word "immoral" in this precept. It seems to me evident that every day each one of us fails, in all kinds of small matters, to proportion precisely our belief to the weight of the evidence. Surely we do not want to say that we are acting immorally in all these cases. I would rephrase the proportionality precept in the following way: In matters of great importance, it is seriously mistaken and often even immoral not to proportion belief in a proposition to the evidence for the proposition. Since I would regard the question of religious faith to be a matter of great importance, this restatement of the proportionality precept will not affect the logic of the discussion that follows.

Premise 2:   Catholicism requires the absolute adherence to some propositions for which there does not exist compelling evidence.   Sullivan frequently repeats the point that many, if not most, other religions could be substituted for Catholicism in this second premise.

Sullivan's defense of religious faith against the *a priori* objection consists of conceding premise 2 and attacking premise 1.   In what follows I will attempt to show that Sullivan's attack on (1) does not succeed, and why I am convinced that (2) is false.   In other words, my claim is that the *a priori* objection can be defeated by defeating (2).   Therefore, the fact that I know of no successful argument against (1) does not disturb me.   Moreover, it is my inclination not only to accept (1) (as I have reformulated it) but to embrace it. Without it, it seems to me, all kinds of sheer folly in important matters gets licensed.

Let's look at Sullivan's attack on Premise 1.   In a vague and general way it's easy to understand what Sullivan is trying to do.   He correctly points out that it is often possible for us to have certainty in the moral or practical domain based upon uncertainty in the speculative domain.   This seems to point out a promising line of defense of religious faith for someone who accepts Premise 2.   One might be able to argue that, despite the lack of sufficient evidence for various religious propositions, one nevertheless has an obligation to accept them with certainty.   We can easily think of examples where doubts concerning the facts nevertheless lead to certainty concerning one's obligations.   If while hunting I have doubts as to whether the movement in the trees is caused by an elk or by a human being, it is clear that I have an obligation not to shoot.   The facts are unclear, the obligation is clear.

Examples could be multiplied.   However, the promise that such examples seem to give for the defense of religious faith against the *a priori* objection vanishes, it seems to me, upon closer inspection of these and similar examples.   Notice that the example does not have the form of going from doubts about proposition X to a clear obligation to believe proposition X. Rather, doubt about one proposition leads to certainty about another proposition. One doubts whether it is an elk or a human being in the trees. One is thereby certain that one should not shoot. The latter certainty does not alter one's doubt about who is in the trees. To reply to the *a priori* objection, Sullivan would have to argue differently. He needs to argue that doubt about religious propositions can precisely form a basis for a compelling obligation to believe those very same religious propositions. As we shall see, it is my position that reasonable doubt about "X" never leads to an obligation to believe "X" with certainty, unless there is further evidence. And the further evidence would be precisely of the type that would remove reasonable doubt about "X".

Sullivan's attack on Premise 1 takes the well known logical form of raising counterexamples to Premise 1. I will argue that his primary counterexample does not work, and that much less does his version of how one comes to religious faith serve as a successful counterexample.

Sullivan offers the following as his primary counterexample. Imagine you are a juror in a civil trial between Smith and Jones. Smith tells his side of the story. When Smith has concluded, and before Jones begins, all the evidence you have heard is on Smith's side. Should you, therefore, proportion your judgment to the evidence as thus far presented and decide that Smith is right? Of course not, Sullivan correctly answers. He then claims that the example is an exception to the proportionality precept. But surely it is not. Among the evidence a juror has at his disposal during such a trial is the evidence that Jones is about to present another side of the story. Therefore, I would say, when one withholds judgment until Jones is heard, one is proportioning one's assent to the evidence that there is more evidence. On the contrary, if one rashly jumps to conclusions without having first heard Jones, one's assent is disproportionate to the evidence that there is more evidence.

By pointing this out I am not claiming that one has an obligation to defer judgment until one is certain that absolutely all the evidence is in. I am only saying that in a case like the one described by Sullivan, there is evidence that new evidence will be quickly forthcoming. And that it would, therefore, be disproportionate to that evidence to judge prematurely.

Sullivan places a tremendous weight on this one counterexample. He believes that by it he has disproved the proportionality precept. He quickly moves on to some general remarks about the relationship between speculative knowledge and practical judgment, gleaning some of them from Newman's *Grammar of Assent*. But all of these remarks are simply question begging unless the proportionality precept has first been defeated. It would seem then that Sullivan believes this one attempted counterexample has done the job. I think it is quite clear that it has not.

Nor is Sullivan's own argument for religious conviction itself a counterexample to the proportionality precept. N1 of this argument says: "If it seems (highly) probable both that an end is obligatory and an action is indispensable to the end, then the action is itself obligatory." Premise N3 says: "It may seem (highly) probable to someone (properly disposed to hear the evidence) that God has revealed that a certain end is an obligatory end (union with Himself) and an action indispensable (absolute adherence to His teachings)." It is precisely at these two premises that we can see that the argument is not a counterexample to the proportionality precept.

Suppose we replaced Premise N3 with N3B: It may seem highly probable to someone that God has revealed that the image of Theodore Roosevelt on Mount Rushmore is to be worshipped, and that therefore the action of going to South Dakota is indispensable. Or we could substitute N3C: It may seem highly probable to someone that God has revealed that baldness is obligatory, and the action of shaving his or her head scrupulously every day is indispensable. Fatuous examples of N3 can be multiplied endlessly. An argument in defense of religious faith that can be used in support of even the zaniest religious conviction would seem to offer little consolation to the Christian believer. Surely both Sullivan and Newman thought they were achieving more than this.

What is the needed antidote? Well, I'm afraid it's just the proportionality precept itself. Why are we inclined to have a low opinion of the religious convictions expressed in N3B and N3C? Because it is not sufficient to justify one's religious convictions to claim that it seems to one that one has an obligation to have those convictions. It is also necessary that one have sufficient grounds for believing one has such an obligation. But to say this is to say that one must have grounds proportionate to the conviction that one has such an obligation. But this is just the proportionality precept back again. We do not respect the obligations expressed in N3B and N3C because we are likely to believe that there are no proportional grounds for such obligations. And so we are still lacking a counterexample for the proportionality precept. If one believes one has an obligation without proportionate evidence in support of that obligation, then one is mistaken— just as the proportionality precept tells us. If in a serious matter it seems to someone that he has a serious obligation, but he has no proportionate evidence for that obligation, then he is seriously mistaken and indeed may be even acting immorally. The proportionality precept is still standing.

Sullivan claims that his defense of religious faith is not just another version of Pascal's wager argument. He claims that it is not a wager argument, because there is genuine probability on one side. But this does not keep it from being a wager. There are various kinds of wagers. There are probabilities involved in football games, horse races, and blackjack. And yet people wager on these all the time. If Sullivan believes that he would be obliged to be uncomfortable if his argument were a wager argument, then I would say that he should be uncomfortable.

Let me summarize my argument to this point. 1) Sullivan has presented no successful counterexample to the proportionality precept; 2) He has presented no other successful argument against the proportionality precept; 3) Without such a counterexample or argument, his attempt to defend religious faith from the *a priori* objection fails.

Conceding that Premise 1 of the *a priori* objection to religious faith is intact, I will now give my own reasons for claiming premise 2 is false. I will maintain, in other words, that the evidence for accepting various religious propositions is indeed compelling.

By what canons of evidence is it compelling? Many of those who accept Premise 2 limit the canon of evidence to that of contemporary natural science. Since Christians believe that coming to knowledge through faith involves the action of the Holy Spirit, they are clearly appealing to evidence that goes beyond that which science accepts. To let the latter set the standard for evidence would be to beg the question against the possibility of knowledge through Christian faith. Sullivan, Newman, Aquinas, and I agree that the evidential base for accepting articles of faith must be wider than the base acceptable in the natural sciences.

Sullivan argues that Premise 2 should be accepted. His argument has two parts. First he goes on at some length to show that natural theology does not provide the evidence for faith. I entirely agree with him on this point and have said so elsewhere ("Reformed Epistemology", *Thomistic Papers IV*, 1988, 185-205). Secondly, he asserts that the evidence for religious faith is not proportionate. But asserting this seems to be nothing more than begging the question in favor of Premise 2. The only support he offers for this assertion is a refrain that he apparently takes to be self-evident, that "faith is not knowledge." But Aquinas, I, and many others would insist that religious faith precisely does give knowledge. It does not, therefore, seem very helpful for Sullivan to assume the opposite in defense of Premise 2.

When I pointed this out to Sullivan in conversation, he conceded that Aquinas grants that faith gives knowledge, but that Aquinas believed knowledge based on faith was less than scientific knowledge. Sullivan has added a footnote to that effect which cites *Questiones Disputatae de Veritate*, question 14, as follows: "Faith is said to be less than scientific knowledge because faith, unlike science, lacks vision of the fact, though it has the same firmness".

But this quote from Aquinas does not help Sullivan. Rather it precisely makes my point. I would interpret Aquinas as meaning the following: Faith knowledge is in some ways less than scientific knowledge, but it may nevertheless be fully compelling. Let me give an example. Suppose the doctors and staff in M. D. Anderson Hospital (famous cancer hospital in Houston) put me through a number of tests and tell me, as a result of these tests, that the evidence conclusively shows that I have lung cancer. This is a situation of faith. That is, it is a situation which calls upon me to trust their word, their testimony as to the facts. Now let's suppose a different case in which I am an oncologist and conduct the biopsy, read the X-rays, and do all the other diagnostic work myself, on my own case. In this case I see all the evidence for myself and am in a position to evaluate it for myself. It seems to me that Aquinas would be right to say that knowledge based upon the testimony of doctors and staff is less than knowledge based upon my own scientific investigation. But this does not mean that the former type of evidence is not fully compelling. Indeed, I think most of us would agree that it would be irrational for someone to refuse to believe that he has lung cancer after repeated tests and repeated reliable testimony insist that he does. So Sullivan may quite rightly say that faith knowledge is not the same as scientific knowledge, but he is wrong to assume that this difference means that faith knowledge is not, or cannot be, fully compelling.

I conclude that Sullivan's defense of Premise 2 does not succeed. He rightly argues that natural theology does not provide a basis for faith knowledge, but this does not prove that there is no other proportionate evidence for faith knowledge. Secondly, his repeated assertion that faith is not knowledge, when revised to mean only that faith knowledge is not scientific knowledge, does not in any way undermine the compelling nature of faith knowledge.   It leaves open, in other words, the possibility that the evidence for faith knowledge is fully compelling, which in turn leaves open the possibility that Premise 2 is false.

Now, perhaps Sullivan would like to reply to my criticism in the following way. He could grant that the proportionality precept (premise 1) holds, and then, still in the spirit of his own argument, attack premise 2.   He could say that, while there is no compelling evidence to accept religious propositions with certainty, there is compelling evidence for an *obligation* to accept religious propositions with certainty.   I have already said that I believe the correct reply to the *a priori* argument against religious belief is to attack premise 2 rather than premise 1.   To this extent Sullivan and I would now be in agreement. I'm afraid, however, that this newfound agreement would not carry us very far.

Let me explain why.   (In what follows I will attribute to Sullivan(?) the above reply, since I have no assurance that the real Sullivan would accept it.)

Sullivan(?) maintains that we can *have* proportionate (compelling) evidence for an *obligation* to accept Proposition X with certainty while at the same time knowing that we do *not* have proportionate (compelling) evidence for simply *accepting* Proposition X with certainty.   I want to examine whether this makes sense, given what we know about human psychology.   Let's suppose, for the sake of argument, that I am convinced that I have an obligation to accept with certainty that for which I know I do not have proportionate evidence.   Would I be able to do it?   Is it possible for me to accept with certainty a proposition while at the very same time knowing that the evidence for the proposition is not proportionate to my accepting it with certainty? I think not. If I am right, and it is impossible to do this, then no amount of obligation to do it would enable me to do it. Indeed, what we must surely say is that, if it is impossible to do it, there cannot be an obligation to do it.

Perhaps Sullivan(?) would reply that, given such an obligation to accept that for which there is not proportionate evidence, one would be obliged to put out of one's mind the fact that there is not proportionate evidence. Having put out of one's mind the fact that there is not proportionate evidence, one might then be psychologically capable of accepting Proposition X with certainty on the strength of a supposed obligation to do so. Let's suppose that one has done this, that one has fulfilled one's obligation to accept "X" with certainty partly by putting out of one's mind the fact that the evidence for accepting "X" with certainty is not proportionate. But let's suppose that after a while the fact that the evidence is not proportionate comes back to mind, and when it is back in mind one is no longer able to assent to Proposition X with certitude. It would follow that one is thereby acting immorally because one is not fulfilling the obligation to accept "X" with certainty. But then one would have failed in one's moral obligations simply by letting a true aspect of the total situation come to mind. This conclusion seems quite absurd to me.

I would say that such a twisted and probably incoherent obligation is contrary to the notion of a good God. On such grounds I would deny that God is or could be the author of such an obligation.

I will now state briefly how I think knowledge by faith comes about and how it serves as a counterexample to Premise 2. Through exposure to evidence in the Scriptures, in the lives of the saints, in the history of the Church, etc., etc., the believer is able, *by the help of the Holy Spirit*, to recognize that, or to arrive at the insight that, God is revealing through these means. With the recognition of a revealing God, the evidence becomes compelling for the acceptance of any propositions thus revealed. The result is faith knowledge based upon the credibility of God's testimony. The role of the Holy Spirit is precisely crucial here. The Holy Spirit enlightening our minds makes available to us evidence that we would otherwise miss or fail to understand deeply enough. Such faith knowledge can grow and mature, become deeper and richer over time. It is also possible that one may at times be tempted by doubt. From the viewpoint of one who has indeed recognized, by the help of the Holy Spirit, the revealing God, these doubts can be seen as unreasonable and dismissed accordingly. One has an obligation to turn away from these doubts precisely because they are unreasonable. Notice the difference between this turning away from doubt and the turning away from doubt that seems to be required by Sullivan(?)'s defense of religious faith. Sullivan(?) claimed that the doubts were reasonable. This made it impossible for us to imagine an obligation to turn away from them. In my view, by contrast, the evidence is compelling by the help of the Holy Spirit, and therefore the doubts are unreasonable. An obligation to turn away from unreasonable doubts is an obligation I think we have no difficulty understanding.

University of St. Thomas
Houston, Texas

By prior agreement, Sullivan was granted space for a final, brief rejoinder.

A REPLY TO RUSSMAN

Thomas D. Sullivan

Given what Russman thinks I hold, he has been very kind to me in his comments. He will perhaps be relieved to know I wouldn't dream of holding the view he refutes. Following Aquinas and Newman, I hold that absolute adherence to a religious teaching makes sense even when we do not have compelling evidence of its truth or the fact that it has been revealed. Russman construes me as arguing that doubt about a religious proposition is the very ground for accepting it as certain. This would be a foolish thing to say—how could ignorance of a proposition serve as a premise for accepting it as certain?—but this is not what I said. I did and do argue that *although* we are in part ignorant, we nonetheless have enough evidence to warrant making the act which God inspires. But the statement "Although p, nonetheless q" is worlds removed from the statement "Because p, therefore q." If you say "*Although* Smith lacks the desired experience, we ought to hire him," do you mean that *because* Smith lacks experience we ought to hire him?

The absurdity of the view Russman mistakes for my thesis induces him to try to reply to the *A Priori* argument along lines I considered but dismissed in the paper. Instead of

joining with me in the rejection of (1), the Proportionality
Precept, Russman tries to reject (2), the claim that Catholicism
requires absolute adherence to some propositions for which there
does not exist compelling evidence.

It is a testimony to Russman's strong faith that he thinks
"The believer is able, *by the help of the Holy Spirit*, to recognize
that, or to arrive at the insight that, God is revealing through
these means," (89) and that all "doubts can be seen as unreasonable."
(Russman, 90).   But this won't do at all as a reason to
reject (2).

Let me explain what I mean.   The faith of many Christians
may be so strong that for them all objections are simply "unreasonable."
One thinks, for example, of St. Teresa in *The Interior Castle*
where she speaks of God implanting Himself in the interior
of a soul in such a way that the soul cannot possibly doubt
that God has been in it.   But if God by His grace sometimes
so illuminates the evidence that He is revealing Himself directly
or through the Church that the soul is *compelled* to accept
the truth, it scarcely follows that every Catholic must be so
favored for faith to be justified.   It is one thing to say the
believer is *able* to arrive at an insight or that all doubts *can*
be seen as unreasonable, quite another to say the illumined
evidence *must* present itself as compelling.   To contradict the
claim that the Church requires absolute adherence in the absence
of compelling evidence, Russman has to claim that the Church
teaches that faith is required of a person only if the evidence
for revelation compels the individual's belief. It won't at all
do just to say that this is the way it does appear to some
people.   One must go further and say "If you don't see as
irrational all objections to the claim that God has revealed
his truth through Christ and the Church, you needn't be a
Catholic."

Of course the Church says no such thing.   Newman, I
say, has it exactly right, and I am convinced—partly because
I once stood in Mrs. Ward's position—that it is crucial to

convey his advice to potential converts. "The simple question then with you is: Have you sufficient grounds for being convinced that the Catholic Church is from God?—If you have, it is nothing to the purpose that you find it difficult to believe— of course it is, for belief is a supernatural act; you must pray to God for the will to believe—for the will has the power to command the mind." (*Letters and Diaries*, Vol. XII, 290).

To insist that God illumines the matter compellingly is to make difficulties for those considering the faith; it is also to make it harder—harder than the Church makes it—to stay within the fold. Jones is out of work, his son has had an emotional breakdown, his wife has cancer. Jones confronts the problem of evil in a way that seriously tests his faith. But he refuses to doubt. Is this not enough? Is he wrong if he clings to his belief though at the moment the evidence seems anything but compelling? When a man with such sorrows retains his Christian faith, are we really to think that by the help of the Holy Spirit the man *sees* that God is revealing himself? Does he believe because God lights up the evidence so that it is *irresistible*, so that all "doubts can be seen as unreasonable?" Or is it not rather, as Newman might say, that the man has successfully endured a trial of his affections?

Russman and I agree that faith is rational only if there exists strong evidence for what it proposes. He goes too far, however, in claiming that the evidence must be compelling. Compelling evidence, as he says, renders all doubt unreasonable. That's the kind of evidence I have for the claim that some humans live on Earth. It would be insane to say otherwise. But is this the way it must be for us if our Catholic faith is to be justified? I hope not. For I must say I possess no such evidence, nor do any I know. (I'm unacquainted with any St. Teresa.) To me not every objection seems just irrational; after thirty years of thinking about some objections I cannot reply entirely to my satisfaction—or to Russman's. What should I do, just pretend to myself that all objections

are inane?   Or should I not rather acknowledge difficulties
as difficulties?   I'm not saying we cannot be as legitimately
certain of religious teaching as we are of truths for which
there is compelling evidence.   Nor am I saying that only
scientific evidence counts. Rather, I am saying that the evidence,
even as illumined by the gift of faith, ordinarily does not
compel assent. Therefore the source of the certainty is ultimately
the will, as moved by grace.   I may believe while recognizing
difficulties because, as Newman has said, a thousand difficulties
do not add up to a single doubt, and I properly refrain from
doubting Catholic truth because the case is good enough to
see that I ought to believe it.   The doctrine is beautiful and
good.   The evidence for its truth is strong.   God calls.   By
His grace, I respond with firm assent.   I do not wait for
the invitation to be His friend to be written on the face of
the sun.

      Proposition (2), then, is true.   The Church does indeed
require belief of those who do not have compelling evidence.
No church authority I have ever read denies this—including
St. Thomas.   For Aquinas, as for Newman, "Faith does not
convince the mind or argue it so as to assent because of
the evidence of the thing, but because of the influence of
the will."   ["(F)ides non convincit sive arguit mentem ex rei
evidentia, sed ex inclinatione voluntatis...." (*Disp. Quest. de
Veritate*, q. 14, a. 2, ad 14).]   The point of the text I cited
from *Quest. Disp. de Veritate* (q. 14, a. 2), is that faith can
be called knowledge only insofar as it shares with knowledge
firmness of belief; unlike knowledge "faith lacks vision of the
fact."   What does this mean but that we do *not* see that
it is so?   It is hard to understand how Russman can draw
support from this passage for his contention that the faithful
do see that what is believed is so.   Unless we want to empty
the Church, we had better not start telling people they lack
the faith if they fail to see the claims of Catholicism bathed
in paradisiacal light of such clarity that all objections display
themselves as absurd.

This, then, is why I cannot accept Russman's way out. But what of mine—or more accurately Newman's and Aquinas'? Has not Russman shown it is equally laden with difficulties?

Not that I can see. Curiously, at the outset he actually says he agrees that (1) as stated is false. Remarking on "[a] small quibble" with my use of the word "immoral" in setting out the Proportionality Precept (1) Russman writes: "It seems to me evident that every day each one of us fails, in all kinds of small matters, to proportion precisely our belief to the weight of the evidence. Surely we do not want to say that we are acting immorally in all these cases." Surely not. So we agree on at least this much—(1) as stated is false. 'Immoral,' I should note, is not a word I plucked from the air; it's the language of W. K. Clifford and others who insist on (1). Russman's "little quibble" is with them, not me.

Russman worries that if we reject (1), as he amends it, then there is no way to fend off even fanatical beliefs. But there is—by producing evidence. Admittedly, we are in no position to say that those who hold false beliefs are immoral. There is, however, such a thing as being wrong, even wildly wrong, in good conscience.

Indeed, one of *us* must be wrong. Happily, not about the faith itself, but about how to answer an objection to it. That in itself should give us pause before accepting the notion that to have the faith is to see all objections to it as irrational.

College of St. Thomas
St. Paul, Minnesota

By prior agreement, Russman was not permitted a further reply.

OTHER PUBLICATIONS OF
THE CENTER FOR THOMISTIC STUDIES

100 Years of Thomism
Victor B. Brezik, C.S.B., ed.
Articles by Henry Veatch, Vernon Bourke, James Weisheipl, Victor
Brezik, Anton Pegis, and Joseph Owens

Thomistic Papers I
Victor B. Brezik, C.S.B., ed.
Articles by Henry Veatch, Vernon Bourke, James Weisheipl, Victor
Brezik, Anton Pegis, and Joseph Owens.

Thomistic Papers II
Leonard A. Kennedy, C.S.B., and Jack C. Marler, eds.
Articles by Laurence Shook, Desmond FitzGerald, Robert Henle,
Francis Kovach, Joseph Owens, and Frederick Wilhelmsen.

Thomistic Papers III
Leonard A. Kennedy, C.S.B., ed.
Articles by Joseph Owens, Edward Synan, Benedict Ashley, Bernard
Doering, and Gerry Lessard.

Thomistic Papers IV
Leonard A. Kennedy, C.S.B., ed.
Articles by Henry Veatch, Henri DuLac, Thomas D. Sullivan, Dennis
Q. McInerny, Richard J. Connell, Joseph Boyle, and Thomas A.
Russman.

Wisdom from St. Augustine
Vernon J. Bourke
Fourteen very readable articles gathered from many periodicals.

About Beauty: A Thomistic Interpretation
Armand A. Maurer, C.S.B.
Beauty and existence, the perception of beauty, beauty and the birth
of the universe, beauty and the human person, beauty and art, beauty
and God.

An Interpretation of Existence
Joseph Owens, C.Ss.R.
The problem of existence, our grasp of existence, the characteristics of existence, the bestowal of existence, the meaning of existence.

An Elementary Christian Metaphysics
Joseph Owens, C.Ss.R.
Being, essence, knowledge, and the immaterial.

A Catalogue of Thomists, 1270-1900
Leonard A. Kennedy, C.S.B.
The names and works of over 2,000 writers with a Thomist reputation, arranged by century, country, and (where applicable) religious community.

Known From the Things That Are
Fundamental Theory of the Moral Life
Martin D. O'Keefe, S.J.
A theoretical and applied treatment of ethics, suitable as an introductory college text using a natural law orientation.

Substance and Modern Science
Richard J. Connell
Avoiding traditional philosophical terminology, this book shows how the notion of substance is valid in modern chemistry, physics, and biology.

All publications of the Center should be ordered from:
University of Notre Dame Press
Notre Dame, Indiana 46556